His Divine Grace
A. C. Bhaktivedanta Swami Prabhupāda
Founder-*Ācārya* of
the International Society for Krishna Consciousness

The Supreme Absolute Truth is the Personality of Godhead, Śrī Kṛṣṇa. His transcendental form is full of eternity, knowledge and bliss. *(p. 1)*

Lord Kṛṣṇa is the creator of all spiritual and material worlds. While Mahā-Viṣṇu, an expansion of Kṛṣṇa, sleeps within the Causal Ocean, He breathes out innumerable universes, and a further expansion, Garbhodakaśāyī Viṣṇu, enters into each universe. *(p. 5)*

Within the material universes, living beings undergo the cycle of repeated birth and death, or reincarnation. But one who understands his relationship with the Supreme Person attains immortality. *(p. 11)*

The self-realized sage sees that the Supreme Person enters into the hearts of all living beings as the Supersoul. Despite external differences, he sees all creatures with equal vision. *(p. 29)*

The perfect *yogī* meditates upon the Personality of Godhead as the Supreme Enjoyer. After giving up his material body, such a *yogī* joins the Supreme Lord in His eternal abode. *(p. 79)*

Lord Kṛṣṇa resides in the topmost spiritual planet, which resembles the whorl of a huge lotus flower. Unlimited other spiritual planets are situated in the effulgence of Kṛṣṇa's planet. The material universes occupy one small portion of the spiritual sky. *(p. 85)*

In His spiritual abode, the Supreme Personality of Godhead performs His transcendental pastimes with His eternal associates, such as the cowherd boys of Vṛndāvana. *(p. 91)*

Śrī Īśopaniṣad

DISCOVERING THE ORIGINAL PERSON

BOOKS by
His Divine Grace
A. C. Bhaktivedanta Swami Prabhupāda

Bhagavad-gītā As It Is
Śrīmad-Bhāgavatam, cantos 1–10 (30 vols.)
Śrī Caitanya-caritāmṛta (17 vols.)
Teachings of Lord Caitanya
The Nectar of Devotion
The Nectar of Instruction
Śrī Īśopaniṣad
Easy Journey to Other Planets
Kṛṣṇa Consciousness: The Topmost Yoga System
Kṛṣṇa, the Supreme Personality of Godhead (3 vols.)
Perfect Questions, Perfect Answers
Dialectical Spiritualism—A Vedic View of Western Philosophy
Teachings of Lord Kapila, the Son of Devahūti
Transcendental Teachings of Prahlād Mahārāja
Teachings of Queen Kuntī
Kṛṣṇa, the Reservoir of Pleasure
The Science of Self-Realization
The Path of Perfection
Search for Liberation
Life Comes From Life
The Perfection of Yoga
Beyond Birth and Death
On the Way to Kṛṣṇa
Geetār-gan (Bengali)
Vairāgya-vidyā (Bengali)
Buddhi-yoga (Bengali)
Bhakti-ratna-bolī (Bengali)
Rāja-vidyā: The King of Knowledge
Elevation to Kṛṣṇa Consciousness
Kṛṣṇa Consciousness: The Matchless Gift
Back to Godhead magazine (founder)

A complete catalog is available upon request.

Bhaktivedanta Book Trust
3764 Watseka Avenue
Los Angeles, California 90034

Śrī Īśopaniṣad

DISCOVERING THE ORIGINAL PERSON

His Divine Grace
A.C. Bhaktivedanta Swami Prabhupāda
Founder-Ācārya of the International Society for Krishna Consciousness

THE BHAKTIVEDANTA BOOK TRUST
Los Angeles · London · Paris · Bombay · Sydney

Readers interested in the subject matter of this book are invited by the International Society for Krishna Consciousness to visit any ISKCON center worldwide (see address list in back of book) or to correspond with the Secretary:

International Society for Krishna Consciousness
3764 Watseka Avenue
Los Angeles, California 90034

First Printing, 1972: 20,000 copies
Second Printing, 1972: 60,000 copies
Third Printing, 1973: 100,000 copies
Fourth Printing, 1973: 100,000 copies
Fifth Printing, 1974: 100,000 copies
Sixth Printing, 1974: 100,000 copies
Seventh Printing, 1975: 300,000 copies
Eighth Printing, 1976: 300,000 copies
Ninth Printing, 1976: 50,000 copies
Tenth Printing, 1982: 300,000 copies
Eleventh Printing, 1982: 150,000 copies

Printed in the United States of America

Library of Congress Catalog Card Number: 78-102853
International Standard Book Number: 0-912776-04-8

Contents

Introduction *vii*
Invocation 1

Mantra One 5
Mantra Two 11
Mantra Three 15
Mantra Four 19
Mantra Five 23
Mantra Six 29
Mantra Seven 33
Mantra Eight 37
Mantra Nine 43
Mantra Ten 49
Mantra Eleven 55
Mantra Twelve 63
Mantra Thirteen 69
Mantra Fourteen 79
Mantra Fifteen 85
Mantra Sixteen 91
Mantra Seventeen 97
Mantra Eighteen 107

Appendixes

The Author 113
Glossary 117
Sanskrit Pronunciation Guide 121
Index of Sanskrit Verses 125
General Index 127

Introduction

"Teachings of the *Vedas*"

[Delivered as a lecture by His Divine Grace A. C. Bhaktivedanta Swami Prabhupāda on October 6, 1969, at Conway Hall, London, England.]

Ladies and gentlemen, today's subject matter is the teachings of the *Vedas*. What are the *Vedas*? The Sanskrit verbal root of *veda* can be interpreted variously, but the purpose is finally one. *Veda* means "knowledge." Any knowledge you accept is *veda*, for the teachings of the *Vedas* are the original knowledge. In the conditioned state our knowledge is subjected to many deficiencies. The difference between a conditioned soul and a liberated soul is that the conditioned soul has four kinds of defects. The first defect is that he must commit mistakes. For example, in our country Mahatma Gandhi was considered to be a very great personality, but he committed many mistakes. Even at the last stage of his life, his assistant warned, "Mahatma Gandhi, don't go to the New Delhi meeting. I have some friends, and I have heard there is danger." But he did not hear. He persisted in going and was killed. Even great personalities like Mahatma Gandhi, President Kennedy—there are so many of them—make mistakes. To err is human. This is one defect of the conditioned soul.

Another defect: to be illusioned. Illusion means to accept something which is not: *māyā*. *Māyā* means "what is not." Everyone is accepting the body as the self. If I ask you what you are, you will say, "I am Mr. John, I am a rich man, I am this, I am that." All these are bodily identifications. But you are not this body. This is illusion.

The third defect is the cheating propensity. Everyone has the propensity to cheat others. Although a person is fool number one, he poses himself as very intelligent. Although it is already pointed out that he is in illusion and makes mistakes, he will theorize, "I think this is this, this is this." But he does not even know his own position. He writes books of philosophy, although he is defective. That is his disease. That is cheating.

Lastly, our senses are imperfect. We are very proud of our eyes. Often someone will challenge, "Can you show me God?" But do you have the eyes to see God? You will never see if you haven't the eyes. If immediately the room becomes dark, you cannot even see your hands. So what power do you have to see? We cannot, therefore, expect knowledge (*veda*) with these imperfect senses. With all these deficiencies in conditioned life, we cannot give perfect knowledge to anyone. Nor are we ourselves perfect. Therefore we accept the *Vedas* as they are.

You may call the *Vedas* Hindu, but Hindu is a foreign name. We are not Hindus. Our real identification is *varṇāśrama. Varṇāśrama* denotes the followers of the *Vedas*, those who accept the human society in eight divisions of *varṇa* and *āśrama*. There are four divisions of society and four divisions of spiritual life. This is called *varṇāśrama*. It is stated in *Bhagavad-gītā*, "These divisions are everywhere, because they are created by God." The divisions of society are *brāhmaṇa*, *kṣatriya*, *vaiśya*, and *śūdra*. *Brāhmaṇa* refers to the very intelligent class of men, those who know what is Brahman. Similarly, the *kṣatriyas*, the administrator group, are the next-intelligent class of men; then the *vaiśyas*, the mercantile group. These natural classifications are found everywhere. This is the Vedic principle, and we accept it. Vedic principles are accepted as axiomatic truth, for there cannot be any mistake. That is acceptance. For instance, in India cow dung is accepted as pure, and yet cow dung is the stool of an animal. In one place you'll find the Vedic injunction that if you touch stool, you have to take a bath immediately. But in another place it is said that the stool of a cow is pure. If you smear cow dung in an impure place, that place becomes pure. With our ordinary sense we can argue, "This is contradictory." Actually, it *is* contradictory from the ordinary point of view, but it is not false. It is fact. In Calcutta, a very prominent scientist and doctor analyzed cow dung and found that it contains all antiseptic properties.

In India if one person tells another, "You must do this," the other party may say, "What do you mean? Is this a Vedic injunction that I have to follow you without any argument?" Vedic injunctions cannot be interpreted. But ultimately, if you carefully study why these injunctions are there, you will find that they are all correct.

The *Vedas* are not compilations of human knowledge. Vedic knowledge comes from the spiritual world, from Lord Kṛṣṇa. Another name for the *Vedas* is *śruti. Śruti* refers to that knowledge that is acquired by hearing. It is not experimental knowledge. *Śruti* is considered to be like a mother. We take so much knowledge from our mother. For example, if you want to know who your father is, who can answer you? Your mother. If the mother says, "Here is your father," you have to accept it. It is not possible to experiment to find out whether he is your father. Similarly, if you want to know something beyond your experience, beyond your experimental knowledge, beyond the activities of the senses, then you have to accept the *Vedas*. There is no question of experimenting. It has already been experimented. It is already settled. The version of the mother, for instance, has to be accepted as truth. There is no other way.

The *Vedas* are considered to be the mother; and Brahmā

is called the grandfather, the forefather, because he was the first to be instructed in the Vedic knowledge. In the beginning the first living creature was Brahmā. He received this Vedic knowledge and imparted it to Nārada and other disciples and sons, and they also distributed it to their disciples. In this way, the Vedic knowledge comes down by disciplic succession. It is also confirmed in the *Bhagavad-gītā* that Vedic knowledge is understood in this way. If you make experimental endeavor you come to the same conclusion, but just to save time you should accept. If you want to know who your father is and if you accept your mother as authority, then whatever she says can be accepted without argument. There are three kinds of evidence: *pratyakṣa*, *anumāna*, and *śabda*. *Pratyakṣa* means "direct." Direct evidence is not very good, because our senses are not perfect. We are seeing the sun daily, and it appears to us just like a small disc, but it is actually far, far larger than many planets. Of what value is this seeing? Therefore we have to read books; then we can understand about the sun. So direct experience is not perfect. Then there is inductive knowledge: "It may be like this," hypothesis. For instance, Darwin's theory says, "It may be like this; it may be like that," but that is not science. That is a suggestion, and it is also not perfect. But if you receive the knowledge from the authoritative sources, that is perfect. If you receive a program guide from the radio station authorities, you accept it. You don't deny it, you don't have to make an experiment, because it is received from the authoritative sources.

Vedic knowledge is called *śabda-pramāṇa*. Another name is *śruti*. *Śruti* means that this knowledge has to be received simply by aural reception. The *Vedas* instruct that in order to understand transcendental knowledge, we have to hear from the authority. Transcendental knowledge is knowledge from beyond this universe. Within this universe is material knowledge, and beyond this universe is transcendental knowledge. We cannot even go to the end of the universe, so how can we go to the spiritual world? Thus to acquire full knowledge is impossible.

There is a spiritual sky. There is another nature, which is beyond manifestation and nonmanifestation. But how will you know that there is a sky where the planets and inhabitants are eternal? All this knowledge is there, but how will you make experiments? It is not possible. Therefore you have to take the assistance of the *Vedas*. This is called Vedic knowledge. In our Kṛṣṇa consciousness movement we are accepting knowledge from the highest authority, Kṛṣṇa. Kṛṣṇa is accepted as the highest authority by all classes of men. I am speaking first of the two classes of transcendentalists. One class of transcendentalist is called impersonalist, Māyāvādī. They are generally known as Vedāntists, led by Śaṅkarācārya. And there is another class of transcendentalists, called Vaiṣṇavas, like Rāmānujācārya, Madhvācārya, Viṣṇusvāmī. Both the Śaṅkara-sampradāya and the Vaiṣṇava-sampradāya have accepted Kṛṣṇa as the Supreme Personality of Godhead. Śaṅkarācārya is supposed to be an impersonalist who preached impersonalism, impersonal Brahman, but it is a fact that he is a covered personalist. In his commentary on the *Bhagavad-gītā* he wrote, "Nārāyaṇa, the Supreme Personality of Godhead, is beyond this cosmic manifestation." And then again he confirmed, "That Supreme Personality of Godhead, Nārāyaṇa, is Kṛṣṇa. He has come as the son of Devakī and Vasudeva." He particularly mentioned the names of His father and mother. So Kṛṣṇa is accepted as the Supreme Personality of Godhead by all transcendentalists. There is no doubt about it. Our source of knowledge in Kṛṣṇa consciousness is directly from Kṛṣṇa, *Bhagavad-gītā*. We have published *Bhagavad-gītā As It Is* because we accept Kṛṣṇa as He is speaking, without any interpretation. That is Vedic knowledge. Since the Vedic knowledge is pure, we accept it. Whatever Kṛṣṇa says, we accept. This is Kṛṣṇa consciousness. That saves much time. If you accept the right authority or source of knowledge, then you save much time. For example, there are two systems of knowledge in the material world—inductive and deductive. From deductive, you accept that man is mortal. Your father says man is mortal, your sister says man is mortal, everyone says man is mortal—but you do not experiment. You accept it as fact that man is mortal. If you want to research to find out whether man is mortal, you have to study each and every man, and you may come to think that there may be some man who is not dying, but you have not seen him yet. So in this way your researching will never be finished. This process is called, in Sanskrit, *āroha*, the ascending process. If you want to attain knowledge by any personal endeavor, by exercising your imperfect senses, you will never come to the right conclusions. That is not possible.

There is a statement in *Brahma-saṁhitā:* Just ride on the airplane that runs at the speed of mind. Our material airplanes can run two thousand miles per hour, but what is the speed of mind? You are sitting at home; you immediately think of India, say ten thousand miles away; and at once it is in your home. Your mind has gone there. The mind speed is so swift. Therefore it is stated, "If you travel at this speed for millions of years, you'll find that the spiritual sky is unlimited." It is not possible even to approach it. Therefore, the Vedic injunction is that one must approach—the word *compulsory* is used—a bona fide spiritual master, a *guru.* And what is the qualification of a spiritual master? He has rightly heard the Vedic message from the right source; otherwise he is not bona fide. And he must practically be firmly established in Brahman. These are the two qualities. This Kṛṣṇa consciousness movement is completely authorized by Vedic principles. In the *Bhagavad-gītā* Kṛṣṇa says, "The actual aim of Vedic research is to find out

Kṛṣṇa." In the *Brahma-saṁhitā* it is also stated, "Kṛṣṇa, Govinda, has innumerable forms, but they are all one." They are not like our forms, which are fallible. His form is infallible. My form has a beginning, but His form has no beginning. It is *ananta.* And His form—so many multiforms—has no end. My form is sitting here and not in my apartment. You are sitting there and not in your apartment. But Kṛṣṇa can be anywhere at one time. He can sit down in Goloka Vṛndāvana, and at the same time He is everywhere, all-pervading. He is original, the oldest, but whenever you look at a picture of Kṛṣṇa you'll find a young boy fifteen or twenty years old. You will never find an old man. You have seen pictures of Kṛṣṇa, as a charioteer, from the *Bhagavad-gītā.* At that time He was not less than one hundred years old. He had great-grandchildren, but He looked just like a boy. Kṛṣṇa, God, never becomes old. That is His supreme power. And if you want to search out Kṛṣṇa by studying the Vedic literature, then you will be baffled. It may be possible, but it is very difficult. But you can very easily learn about Him from His devotee. His devotee can deliver Him to you: "Here He is, take Him." That is the potency of Kṛṣṇa's devotees.

Originally there was only one *Veda,* and there was no necessity of reading it. People were so intelligent and had such sharp memories that by once hearing from the lips of the spiritual master they would understand. They would immediately grasp the whole purport. But five thousand years ago Vyāsadeva put the *Vedas* in writing for the people in this age, Kali-yuga. He knew that eventually the people would be short-lived, their memories would be very poor, and their intelligence would not be very sharp. "Therefore, let me teach this Vedic knowledge in writing." He divided the *Vedas* into four: *Ṛg, Sāma, Atharva,* and *Yajur.* Then he gave the charge of these *Vedas* to his different disciples. He then thought of the less intelligent class of men, *strī*, *śūdra*, and *dvija-bandhu*. He considered the woman class and the *śūdra* class (worker class) and *dvija-bandhu*. *Dvija-bandhu* refers to those who are born in a high family but who are not properly qualified. A man born in the family of a *brāhmaṇa* who is not qualified as a *brāhmaṇa* is called *dvija-bandhu*. For these persons he compiled *Mahābhārata*, called the history of India, and the eighteen *Purāṇas*. These are all Vedic literatures: the *Purāṇas*, the *Mahābhārata*, the four *Vedas*, and the *Upaniṣads*. The *Upaniṣads* are part of the *Vedas*. Then Vyāsadeva summarized all Vedic knowledge for scholars and philosophers in what is called the *Vedānta-sūtra*. This is the last word of the *Vedas*. Vyāsadeva personally wrote *Vedānta-sūtra* under the instructions of Nārada, his *guru-mahārāja*, spiritual master, but still he was not satisfied. That is a long story, described in the *Śrīmad-Bhāgavatam*. Vedavyāsa was not very satisfied even after compiling many *Purāṇas*, *Upaniṣads*, and even after *Vedānta-sūtra*. Then his spiritual master, Nārada, instructed him, "You explain *Vedānta*." *Vedānta* means "ultimate knowledge," and the ultimate knowledge is Kṛṣṇa. Kṛṣṇa says that throughout all the *Vedas* one has to understand Kṛṣṇa. *Vedānta-kṛd veda-vid eva cāham*. Kṛṣṇa says, "I am the compiler of *Vedānta*, and I am the knower of the *Vedas*." Therefore the ultimate objective is Kṛṣṇa. That is explained in all the Vaiṣṇava commentaries on *Vedānta* philosophy. We Gauḍīya Vaiṣṇavas have our commentary on *Vedānta* philosophy, called *Govinda-bhāṣya*, by Baladeva Vidyābhūṣaṇa. Similarly, Rāmānujācārya has a commentary, and Madhvācārya has one. The version of Śaṅkarācārya is not the only commentary. There are many *Vedānta* commentaries; but because the Vaiṣṇavas did not present the first *Vedānta* commentary, people are under the wrong impression that Śaṅkarācārya's is the only *Vedānta* commentary.

Besides that, Vyāsadeva himself wrote the perfect *Vedānta* commentary, *Śrīmad-Bhāgavatam. Śrīmad-Bhāgavatam* also begins with the first words of the *Vedānta-sūtra: janmādy asya yataḥ.* And that *janmādy asya yataḥ* is fully explained in the *Śrīmad-Bhāgavatam.* The *Vedānta-sūtra* simply hints at what is Brahman, the Absolute Truth: "The Absolute Truth is that from whom everything emanates." This is a summary, but it is explained in detail in *Śrīmad-Bhāgavatam.* If everything is emanating from the Absolute Truth, then what is the nature of the Absolute Truth? That is explained in *Śrīmad-Bhāgavatam.* The Absolute Truth must be consciousness. He is self-effulgent (*sva-rāṭ*). We develop our consciousness and knowledge by receiving knowledge from others, but for Him it is said that He is self-effulgent. The whole summary of Vedic knowledge is the *Vedānta-sūtra,* and the *Vedānta-sūtra* is explained by the writer himself in the *Śrīmad-Bhāgavatam.* We finally request those who are actually after Vedic knowledge to try to understand the explanation of all Vedic knowledge from *Śrīmad-Bhāgavatam* and *Bhagavad-gītā.*

INVOCATION

ॐ पूर्णमदः पूर्णमिदं पूर्णात् पूर्णमुदच्यते ।
पूर्णस्य पूर्णमादाय पूर्णमेवावशिष्यते ॥

oṁ pūrṇam adaḥ pūrṇam idaṁ
pūrṇāt pūrṇam udacyate
pūrṇasya pūrṇam ādāya
pūrṇam evāvaśiṣyate

oṁ—the complete whole; *pūrṇam*—perfectly complete; *adaḥ*—that; *pūrṇam*—perfectly complete; *idam*—this phenomenal world; *pūrṇāt*—from the all-perfect; *pūrṇam*—complete unit; *udacyate*—is produced; *pūrṇasya*—of the complete whole; *pūrṇam*—completely, all; *ādāya*—having been taken away; *pūrṇam*—the complete balance; *eva*—even; *avaśiṣyate*—is remaining.

TRANSLATION

The Personality of Godhead is perfect and complete, and because He is completely perfect, all emanations from Him, such as this phenomenal world, are perfectly equipped as complete wholes. Whatever is produced of the complete whole is also complete in itself. Because He is the complete whole, even though so many complete units emanate from Him, He remains the complete balance.

PURPORT

The complete whole, or the Supreme Absolute Truth, is the complete Personality of Godhead. Realization of impersonal Brahman or of Paramātmā, the Supersoul, is incomplete realization of the Absolute Complete. The Supreme Personality of Godhead is *sac-cid-ānanda-vigraha,* and impersonal Brahman realization is the realization of His *sat* feature, or His aspect of eternity; and Paramātmā, or Supersoul, realization is the realization of His *sat* and *cit* features, His aspects of eternity and knowledge. Realization of the Personality of Godhead, however, is realization of all the transcendental features—*sat, cit,* and *ānanda,* bliss. When one realizes the Supreme Person, he realizes these aspects in complete form (*vigraha*). Thus the complete whole is not formless. If He were formless, or if He were any less than His creation in any way, He could not be complete. The complete whole must contain everything, both within and beyond our experience, otherwise He cannot be complete.

The complete whole, the Personality of Godhead, has immense potencies, all of which are as complete as He is. Thus this phenomenal, or material, world is also complete in itself. The twenty-four elements of which this material universe is a temporary manifestation are arranged to produce everything necessary for the maintenance and subsistence of this universe. No other unit in the universe need make an extraneous effort to try to maintain the universe. The universe functions on its own time scale, which is fixed by the energy of the complete whole; and when that time schedule is complete, this temporary manifestation will be annihilated by the complete arrangement of the complete.

All facilities are given to the complete units (namely the living beings) to enable them to realize the complete whole. All forms of incompletion are experienced due to incomplete knowledge of the complete whole. The human form of life is a complete manifestation of the consciousness of the living being, and it is obtained after evolving through 8,400,000 species of life in the cycle of birth and death. If the living entity does not realize his completeness within the complete whole in this human life, which has the benediction of full consciousness, he loses the chance to realize his completeness and is again put into the evolutionary cycle by the law of material nature.

Because we do not know that there is complete arrangement in nature for our maintenance, we make efforts to utilize the resources of nature to create a so-called complete life of sense enjoyment. Because the living entity cannot enjoy the life of the senses without being dovetailed to the complete whole, the misleading life of sense enjoyment is considered illusion. The hand of a body is a complete unit only as long as it is attached to the complete body. When the hand is severed from the body, it may appear like a hand, but it actually has none of the potencies of a hand. Similarly, living beings are parts and parcels of the complete whole, and if they are severed from the complete whole, the illusory representation of completeness cannot fully satisfy them.

The completeness of human life can only be realized when one engages in the service of the complete whole. All services in this world—whether social, political, communal, international, or even interplanetary—will remain incomplete until they are dovetailed with the complete whole. When everything is dovetailed with the complete whole, the attached parts and parcels also become complete in themselves.

MANTRA ONE

ईशावास्यमिदं सर्वं यत्किञ्च जगत्यां जगत् ।
तेन त्यक्तेन भुञ्जीथा मा गृधः कस्य स्विद्धनम् ॥ १ ॥

īśāvāsyam idaṁ sarvaṁ
yat kiñca jagatyāṁ jagat
tena tyaktena bhuñjīthā
mā gṛdhaḥ kasya svid dhanam

īśa—by the Lord; *āvāsyam*—controlled; *idam*—this; *sarvam*—all; *yat kiñca*—whatever; *jagatyām*—within the universe; *jagat*—all that is animate or inanimate; *tena*—by Him; *tyaktena*—set-apart quota; *bhuñjīthāḥ*—you should accept; *mā*—do not; *gṛdhaḥ*—endeavor to gain; *kasya svit*—of anyone else; *dhanam*—the wealth.

TRANSLATION

Everything animate or inanimate that is within the universe is controlled and owned by the Lord. One should therefore accept only those things necessary for himself, which are set aside as his quota, and one should not accept other things, knowing well to whom they belong.

PURPORT

Vedic knowledge is infallible because it comes down through the perfect disciplic succession of spiritual masters beginning with the Lord Himself. The first word of Vedic knowledge was spoken by the Lord Himself, and it is being received from transcendental sources. The words spoken by the Lord are called *apauruṣeya*, which indicates that they are not delivered by any mundane person. A living being who lives in the mundane world has four defects: (1) he is certain to commit mistakes, (2) he is subject to illusion, (3) he has a propensity to cheat others, and (4) his senses are imperfect. Being conditioned by these four imperfections, one cannot deliver perfect information of all-pervading knowledge. The *Vedas* are not produced by such imperfect creatures. Vedic knowledge was originally imparted into the heart of Brahmā, the first created living being, and Brahmā in his turn disseminated this knowledge to his sons and disciples, who have handed down the process through history.

Since the Lord is *pūrṇam*, or all-perfect, there is no possibility of His being subjected to the laws of material nature; however, the living entities and inanimate objects are both controlled by the laws of nature and ultimately by the Lord's potency. This *Īśopaniṣad* is part of the *Yajur Veda*, and consequently it contains information concerning the proprietorship of all things existing within the universe.

This is confirmed in the Seventh Chapter of *Bhagavad-gītā* (7.4–5), where *parā* and *aparā prakṛti* are discussed. The elements of nature—earth, fire, water, air, ether, mind, intelligence, and ego—all belong to the inferior, or material, energy of the Lord, whereas the living being, the organic energy, is the *parā prakṛti* (superior energy) of the Lord. Both of the *prakṛtis*, or energies, are emanations from the Lord, and ultimately He is the controller of everything that exists.

There is nothing in the universe that does not belong either to the *parā* or the *aparā prakṛti;* therefore everything is the property of the Supreme Being.

The Supreme Being, the Absolute Personality of Godhead, is a complete person, and He has complete and perfect intelligence to adjust everything by means of His different potencies. The Supreme Being is often compared to fire, and everything organic and inorganic is compared to the heat and light of that fire. Just as fire distributes energy in the form of heat and light, the Lord displays His energy in different ways. He thus remains the ultimate controller, sustainer, and dictator of everything. He is the knower of everything and the benefactor of everyone. He is full of all inconceivable potencies: power, wealth, fame, beauty, knowledge, and renunciation.

One should therefore be intelligent enough to know that but for the Lord, no one is a proprietor of anything. One should accept only those things that are set aside by the Lord as his quota. The cow, for instance, gives milk, but she does not drink that milk; she eats grass and grain, and her milk is designated as food for human beings. Such is the arrangement of the Lord, and we should be satisfied with those things that He has kindly set aside for us, and we should always consider to whom those things we possess actually belong.

A house, for instance, is made of earth, wood, stone, iron, cement, and so many other material things, and if we think in terms of *Śrī Īśopaniṣad,* we must know that we cannot produce any of these materials ourselves. We can simply bring them together and transform them into different shapes by our labor. A laborer cannot claim to be a proprietor of a thing just because he has worked hard to manufacture it.

In modern society there is always a great quarrel between the laborers and the capitalists. This quarrel has taken an international shape, and the world is endangered. Men face one another in enmity and snarl just like cats and dogs. *Śrī Īśopaniṣad* cannot give advice to the cats and dogs, but it can deliver the message of Godhead to man through the bona fide *ācāryas* (holy teachers). The human race should take the Vedic wisdom of *Īśopaniṣad* and not quarrel over material possessions. One must be satisfied with whatever privileges are given to him by the mercy of the Lord. There can be no peace if the communists or capitalists or any other party claims proprietorship over the resources of nature, which are entirely the property of the Lord. The capitalists cannot curb the communists simply by political maneuvering, nor can the communists defeat the capitalists simply by fighting for stolen bread. If they do not recognize the proprietorship of the Supreme Personality of Godhead, all the property that they claim to be their own is stolen. Consequently they will be liable to punishment by the laws of nature. Nuclear bombs are in the hands of both communists and capitalists, and if both do not recognize the proprietorship of the Supreme Lord, it is certain that these bombs will ultimately ruin both parties. Thus in order to save themselves and bring peace to the world, both parties must follow the instructions of *Śrī Īśopaniṣad.*

Human beings are not meant to quarrel like cats and dogs. They must be intelligent enough to realize the importance and aim of human life. The Vedic literatures are compiled for humanity and not for cats and dogs. Cats and dogs can kill other animals for food without incurring sin, but if a man kills an animal for the satisfaction of his uncontrolled taste buds, he is responsible for breaking the laws of nature. Consequently, he must be punished.

The standard of life for human beings cannot be applied to animals. The tiger does not eat rice, wheat, or drink cow's milk, because he has been given food in the shape of animal flesh. There are many animals and birds that are either vegetarian or carnivorous, but none of them transgress the laws of nature, as these laws have been ordained by the will of God. Animals, birds, reptiles, and other lower life forms strictly adhere to the laws of nature; therefore there is no question of sin for them, nor are the Vedic instructions meant for them. Human life alone is a life of responsibility.

It is wrong to consider that simply by becoming a vegetarian one can avoid transgressing the laws of nature. Vegetables also have life. It is nature's law that one living being is meant to feed another. Thus one should not be proud of being a strict vegetarian; the point is to recognize the Supreme Lord. Animals do not have developed consciousness by which to recognize the Lord, but a human being is sufficiently intelligent to take lessons from Vedic literatures and thereby know how the laws of nature are working and derive profit out of such knowledge. If a man neglects the instructions of the Vedic literatures, his life becomes very risky. A human being is therefore required to recognize the authority of the Supreme Lord. He must be a devotee of the Lord, offer everything to the Lord's service, and partake only of the remnants of food offered to the Lord. This will enable him to discharge his duty properly. In *Bhagavad-gītā* (9.26) the Lord directly states that He accepts vegetarian food from the hands of a pure devotee. Therefore a human being should not only become a strict vegetarian but should also become a devotee of the Lord and offer the Lord all his food. Then only should one partake of *prasāda*, or mercy of God. A devotee who can act in this consciousness can properly discharge the duty of human life. Those who do not offer their food to the Lord actually eat sin and subject themselves to various types of distress, which are the results of sin (Bg. 3.13).

The root of sin is deliberate disobedience to the laws of

nature through disregarding the proprietorship of the Lord. Disobedience to the laws of nature or the order of the Lord brings ruin to a human being. If one is sober, knows the laws of nature, and is not influenced by unnecessary attachment or aversion, he is sure to be recognized by the Lord, and he is sure to become eligible to go back to Godhead, back to the eternal home.

MANTRA TWO

कुर्वन्नेवेह कर्माणि जिजीविषेच्छतꣳ समाः ।
एवं त्वयि नान्यथेतोऽस्ति न कर्म लिप्यते नरे ॥ २ ॥

kurvann eveha karmāṇi
jijīviṣec chataṁ samāḥ
evaṁ tvayi nānyatheto 'sti
na karma lipyate nare

kurvan—doing continuously; *eva*—thus; *iha*—during this span of life; *karmāṇi*—work; *jijīviṣet*—one should desire to live; *śatam*—one hundred; *samāḥ*—years; *evam*—so living; *tvayi*—unto you; *na*—no; *anyathā*—alternative; *itaḥ*—from this path; *asti*—there is; *na*—not; *karma*—work; *lipyate*—can be bound; *nare*—unto a man.

TRANSLATION

One may aspire to live for hundreds of years if he continuously goes on working in that way, for that sort of work will not bind him to the law of karma. There is no alternative to this way for man.

PURPORT

No one wants to die, and everyone wants to live as long as he can drag on. This tendency is not only visible individually but also collectively in the community, society, and nation. There is a hard struggle for life by all kinds of living entities, and the *Vedas* say that this is quite natural. The living being is eternal by nature, but due to his bondage in material existence he has to change his body over and over. This process is called the transmigration of the soul, and this transmigration is due to *karma-bandhana*, or bondage to one's work. The living entity has to work for his livelihood because that is the law of material nature, and if he does not act according to his prescribed duties, he transgresses the law of nature and binds himself more and more to the cycle of birth and death.

Other life forms are also subject to the cycle of birth and death, but when the living entity attains a human life, he gets a chance to get free from the law of *karma*. *Karma*, *akarma*, and *vikarma* are very clearly described in *Bhagavad-gītā*. Actions that are performed in terms of one's prescribed duties, as mentioned in the revealed scriptures, are called *karma*. Actions that free one from the cycle of birth and death are called *akarma*. And actions that are performed by the misuse of one's freedom and that direct one to the lower life forms are called *vikarma*. Of these three types of action, that which frees one from the bondage of *karma* is preferred by intelligent men. Ordinary men wish to perform good works in order to be recognized and achieve some higher status of life in this world or in heaven, but more advanced men want to be free altogether from the actions and reactions of work. Intelligent men know well that both good and bad works equally bind one to the material miseries. Consequently they seek that work that will free them from the reactions of both good and bad work.

The instructions of *Śrī Īśopaniṣad* are more elaborately explained in *Bhagavad-gītā*, sometimes called *Gītopaniṣad*, the cream of all the *Upaniṣads*. In *Bhagavad-gītā* (3.9–16) the Personality of Godhead says that one cannot attain the state of *naiṣkarma* or *akarma* without executing the prescribed duties mentioned in Vedic literatures. The *Vedas* can regulate the working energy of a human being in such a way that one can gradually realize the authority of the Supreme Being. When one realizes the authority of the Personality of Godhead, it is to be understood that he has attained the stage of positive knowledge. In this purified stage the modes of nature—namely goodness, passion, and ignorance—cannot act, and one is enabled to work on the basis of *naiṣkarma*. Such work does not bind one to the cycle of birth and death.

Factually, no one has to do anything more than render devotional service to the Lord. However, in the lower stages of life one cannot immediately adopt the activities of devotional service, nor can one completely stop fruitive work. A conditioned soul is accustomed to working for sense gratification, for his own selfish interest, immediate or extended. An ordinary man works for his own sense enjoyment, and when this principle of sense enjoyment is extended to include his society, nation, or humanity in general, it assumes various attractive names such as altruism, socialism, communism, nationalism, humanitarianism, etc. These *isms* are certainly very attractive forms of *karma-bandhana* ("work which binds"), but the Vedic instruction of *Īśopaniṣad* is that if one actually wants to live for any of the above *isms*, he should make them God-centered. There is no harm in becoming a family man, or an altruist, socialist, communist, nationalist, or humanitarian, provided that one executes his activities in relation with *īśāvāsya*, the God-centered conception.

Bhagavad-gītā (2.40) states that God-centered activities are so valuable that just a few of them can save a person from the greatest danger. The greatest danger of life is the danger of gliding down again into the evolutionary cycle of birth and death. If some way or another a man misses the spiritual opportunity afforded by his human form of life and falls down again into the evolutionary cycle, he must be considered most unfortunate. Due to his defective senses, a foolish man cannot see that this is happening. Consequently, *Śrī Īśopaniṣad* advises us to exert our energy in the spirit of *īśāvāsya.* Being so engaged we may wish to live for many, many years; otherwise, a long life in itself has no value. A tree lives for hundreds and perhaps thousands of years, but there is no point in living a long time like trees, or breathing like bellows, or begetting children like hogs and dogs, or eating like a camel. A humble, God-centered life is more valuable than a colossal hoax of a life dedicated to godless altruism or socialism.

When altruistic activities are executed in the spirit of *Śrī Īśopaniṣad,* they become a form of *karma-yoga.* Such activities are recommended in *Bhagavad-gītā* (18.5–9), for they guarantee their executor protection from the dangers of sliding down into the evolutionary process of birth and death. Even though such God-centered activities may be half-finished, they are still good for the executor, because they will guarantee him a human form in his next birth. In this way one can have another chance to improve his position on the path of liberation.

MANTRA THREE

असुर्या नाम ते लोका अन्धेन तमसाऽऽवृताः ।
ताꣳस्ते प्रेत्याभिगच्छन्ति ये के चात्महनो जनाः ॥ ३ ॥

asuryā nāma te lokā
andhena tamasāvṛtāḥ
tāṁs te pretyābhigacchanti
ye ke cātma-hano janāḥ

asuryāḥ—meant for the *asuras*; *nāma*—famous by the name; *te*—those; *lokāḥ*—planets; *andhena*—by ignorance; *tamasā*—by darkness; *āvṛtāḥ*—covered; *tān*—those planets; *te*—they; *pretya*—after death; *abhigacchanti*—enter into; *ye*—anyone; *ke*—everyone; *ca*—and; *ātma-hanaḥ*—the killers of the soul; *janāḥ*—persons.

TRANSLATION

The killer of the soul, whoever he may be, must enter into the planets known as the worlds of the faithless, full of darkness and ignorance.

PURPORT

A human life is distinguished from animal life due to its heavy responsibilities. Those who are cognizant of these responsibilities and who work in that spirit are called *suras* (godly persons), and those who are neglectful of these responsibilities or who have no information of them are called *asuras* (demons). These two types of human beings are found all over the universe. In the *Ṛg Veda* it is stated that the *suras* always aim at the lotus feet of the Supreme Lord, Viṣṇu, and act accordingly. Their ways are as illuminated as the path of the sun.

Intelligent human beings must always remember that this particular bodily form is obtained after an evolution of many millions of years and after long transmigration. This material world is sometimes compared to an ocean, and this human body is compared to a solid boat designed especially to cross this ocean. The Vedic scriptures and the *ācāryas*, or saintly teachers, are compared to expert boatmen, and the facilities of the human body are compared to favorable breezes which help the boat ply smoothly to its desired destination. If, with all these facilities, a person does not fully utilize his life for self-realization, he must be considered *ātma-hā*, a killer of the soul. *Śrī Īśopaniṣad* gives warning in clear terms that the killer of the soul is destined to enter into the darkest region of ignorance to suffer perpetually.

There are swine, dogs, camels, asses, etc., whose economic necessities are just as important as ours, but the economic problems of these animals are only solved under nasty and unpleasant conditions. The human being is given all facilities for a comfortable life by the laws of nature because the human form of life is more important and valuable than animal life. Why does man have a better life than the swine and other animals? Why is he a highly placed servant, given all facilities, rather than an ordinary clerk? The answer is that a highly placed officer has to discharge duties of a higher nature; a human being has higher duties to perform than animals, who are always engaged in simply feeding their hungry stomachs. Yet modern soul-killing civilization has only increased the problems of a hungry stomach. When we approach a polished animal in the form of modern civilized man and ask him what his business is, he will say that he simply wants to work to satisfy his stomach and that there is no need for self-realization. The laws of nature are so cruel, however, that despite his eagerness to work hard for his stomach, he is always threatened by the question of unemployment.

We are given this human form of life not to work hard like asses and swine, but to attain the highest perfection of life. If we do not care for self-realization, the laws of nature force us to work very hard, even though we may not want to do so. Human beings in this age have been forced to work hard like the asses and bulls that pull carts. Some of the regions where the *asuras* are sent to work are revealed in this verse of *Śrī Īśopaniṣad.* If a man fails to discharge his duties as a human being, he is forced to transmigrate to the *asurya* planets and take birth in degraded species of life to work hard in ignorance and darkness.

In *Bhagavad-gītā* (6.41–43) it is stated that a man who enters upon the path of self-realization but does not complete the process, despite having sincerely tried for it, is given a chance to appear in a family of *śuci* or *śrīmat.* The word *śuci* indicates a spiritually advanced *brāhmaṇa,* and *śrīmat* indicates a *vaiśya,* a member of the mercantile community. This indicates that the person who fails to realize his relation with God is given a better chance to cultivate self-realization, due to his sincere efforts in his previous lives. If even a fallen candidate is given a chance to take birth in a respectable and noble family, one can hardly imagine the status of one who has achieved success. By simply attempting to realize God, one is guaranteed birth in a wealthy or aristocratic family. However, one who does not even make an attempt, who wants to be covered by illusion, who is too materialistic and attached to material enjoyment, must enter into the darkest regions of hell, as confirmed in all Vedic literatures. Such materialistic *asuras* sometimes make a show of religion, but their ultimate aim is material prosperity. *Bhagavad-gītā* (16.17–18) rebukes such men, for they are considered great only on the strength of deception and are empowered by the votes of the ignorant and by their own material wealth. Such *asuras*, devoid of self-realization and knowledge of *īśāvāsya*, the Lord, are certain to enter into the darkest regions.

The conclusion is that as human beings we are not meant for simply solving economic problems on a tottering platform but for solving all the problems of the material life into which we have been placed by the laws of nature.

MANTRA FOUR

अनेजदेकं मनसो जवीयो नैनद्देवा आप्नुवन् पूर्वमर्षत् ।
तद्धावतोऽन्यानत्येति तिष्ठत्तस्मिन्नपो मातरिश्वा दधाति ॥ ४ ॥

anejad ekaṁ manaso javīyo
nainad devā āpnuvan pūrvam arṣat
tad dhāvato 'nyān atyeti tiṣṭhat
tasminn apo mātariśvā dadhāti

anejat—fixed; *ekam*—one; *manasaḥ*—than the mind; *javīyaḥ*—more swift; *na*—not; *enat*—this Supreme Lord; *devāḥ*—the demigods like Indra, etc.; *āpnuvan*—can approach; *pūrvam*—in front; *arṣat*—moving quickly; *tat*—He; *dhāvataḥ*—those who are running; *anyān*—others; *atyeti*—surpasses; *tiṣṭhat*—remaining in one place; *tasmin*—in Him; *apaḥ*—rain; *mātariśvā*—the gods who control the wind and rain; *dadhāti*—supply.

TRANSLATION

Although fixed in His abode, the Personality of Godhead is swifter than the mind and can overcome all others running. The powerful demigods cannot approach Him. Although in one place, He controls those who supply the air and rain. He surpasses all in excellence.

PURPORT

The Supreme Lord, who is the Absolute Personality of Godhead, cannot be known by mental speculation even by the greatest philosopher. He can be known only by His devotees, through His mercy. In *Brahma-saṁhitā* it is stated that even if a nondevotee philosopher travels at the speed of mind for hundreds of years, he will still find the Absolute Truth far, far away from him. As described in the *Īśopaniṣad*, the Absolute Personality of Godhead has His transcendental abode, known as Kṛṣṇaloka, where He remains and engages in His pastimes. Yet by His inconceivable potencies He can simultaneously reach every part of His creative energy. In the *Viṣṇu Purāṇa*, His potencies are compared to the heat and light that emanate from fire. Although situated in one place, a fire can distribute its light and heat all over; similarly, the Absolute Personality of Godhead, although fixed in His transcendental abode, can diffuse His different energies everywhere.

Although His energies are innumerable, they can be divided into three principal categories: the internal potency, the marginal potency, and the external potency. There are hundreds and millions of subheadings to each of these categories. The dominating demigods who are empowered to control and administer natural phenomena such as air, light, rain, etc., are all classified within the marginal potency of the Absolute Person. Living beings, including humans, are also products of the Lord's marginal potency. The material world is the creation of the Lord's external potency, and the spiritual sky, or kingdom of God, is the manifestation of His internal potency.

Thus the different energies of the Lord are present everywhere through His different potencies. Although there is no difference between the Lord and His energies, one should not wrongly consider that the Supreme Lord is distributed everywhere impersonally or that He loses His personal existence. Men are accustomed to reach conclusions according to their capacity to understand, but the Supreme Lord is not subject to our limited capacity for understanding. It is for this reason that the *Upaniṣads* warn us that no one can approach the Lord by his own limited potency.

In *Bhagavad-gītā* (10.2) the Lord says that not even the great *ṛṣis* and *suras* can know Him. And what to speak of the *asuras*, who are not even qualified to understand the ways of the Lord? This fourth *mantra* very clearly suggests that the Absolute Truth is ultimately the Absolute Person; otherwise there would have been no need to mention so much variegatedness in support of His personal features.

Although they have all the symptoms of the Lord Himself, the individual parts and parcels of the Lord's potencies have limited spheres of activity and are therefore all limited. The parts and parcels are never equal to the whole; therefore they cannot appreciate the Lord's full potency. Under the influence of material nature, foolish and ignorant living beings, who are but parts and parcels of the Lord, try to conjecture about the Lord's transcendental position. *Śrī Īśopaniṣad* warns of the futility in trying to establish the identity of the Lord through mental speculation. One should try to learn of transcendence from a superior source like the *Vedas*, which already contain knowledge of transcendence.

Every part of the complete whole is endowed with some particular energy to act. When that part forgets his particular activities, he is considered to be in *māyā*, illusion. Thus from the very beginning, *Śrī Īśopaniṣad* warns us to be very careful to play the part designated for us by the Lord. This does not mean that the individual soul has no initiative of his own. Because he is part and parcel of the Lord, he must partake of the initiative of the Lord as well. When one properly utilizes his initiative or active nature with intelligence, understanding that everything is the Lord's potency, he can revive his original consciousness, which was lost due to association with *māyā*, the external energy.

All power is obtained from the Lord; therefore each particular power must be utilized to execute the will of the Lord and not otherwise. The Lord can be known by one who has adopted a submissive attitude. Perfect knowledge means knowing the Lord in all His features, knowing His potencies, and knowing how these potencies work by His will. These matters are exclusively described by the Lord in *Bhagavad-gītā*, which is the essence of all the *Upaniṣads*.

MANTRA FIVE

तदेजति तन्नैजति तद्दूरे तद्वन्तिके ।
तदन्तरस्य सर्वस्य तदु सर्वस्यास्य बाह्यतः ॥ ५ ॥

tad ejati tan naijati
tad dūre tad v antike
tad antar asya sarvasya
tad u sarvasyāsya bāhyataḥ

tat—this Supreme Lord; *ejati*—walks; *tat*—He; *na*—not; *ejati*—walks; *tat*—He; *dūre*—far away; *tat*—He; *u*—also; *antike*—very near; *tat*—He; *antaḥ*—within; *asya*—of this; *sarvasya*—of all; *tat*—He; *u*—also; *sarvasya*—of all; *asya*—of this; *bāhyataḥ*—external to.

TRANSLATION

The Supreme Lord walks and does not walk. He is far away, but He is very near as well. He is within everything, and yet He is outside of everything.

PURPORT

Here is an explanation of the Supreme Lord's transcendental activities as executed by His inconceivable potencies.

Contradictions are given here by way of proving the inconceivable potencies of the Lord. He walks, and He does not walk. Such a contradiction serves to indicate the inconceivable power of God. With our limited fund of knowledge, we cannot make accommodations for such contradictions; we can only conceive of the Lord in terms of our limited powers of understanding. The impersonalist philosophers of the Māyāvāda school accept only the Lord's impersonal activities and reject His personal feature. The *Bhāgavata* school, however, accepts the Lord as both personal and impersonal. The *bhāgavatas* also accept His inconceivable potencies, for without them there can be no meaning to the words *Supreme Lord.*

We should not take it for granted that just because we cannot see God with our eyes the Lord does not have a personal existence. *Śrī Īśopaniṣad* refutes this argument by warning us that the Lord is far away but very near also. The abode of the Lord is beyond the material sky, and we have no means to measure even this material sky. If the material sky extends so far, then what to speak of the spiritual sky, which is altogether beyond it? That the spiritual sky is situated far, far away from the material universe is also confirmed in *Bhagavad-gītā* (15.6). But despite the Lord's being so far away, He can at once, within less than a second, descend before us with a speed swifter than the mind or the wind. He can also walk so swiftly that no one can surpass Him. This has already been described in the previous verse.

Yet when the Personality of Godhead comes before us, we neglect Him. Such foolish negligence is condemned by the Lord in *Bhagavad-gītā* (9.11), wherein the Lord says that the foolish deride Him when they consider Him to be a mortal being. He is not a mortal being, nor does He come before us with a body produced of material nature. There are many so-called scholars who contend that the Lord descends in a body made of matter, just like an ordinary living being. Not knowing His inconceivable power, such foolish men place the Lord on a level equal to that of ordinary men.

Because He is full of inconceivable potencies, God can accept our service through any sort of medium, and He can convert His different potencies according to His own will. Nonbelievers argue that the Lord cannot incarnate Himself at all, and if He does He descends in a form of material energy. This argument is nullified if we accept the inconceivable potencies of the Lord to be realities. Even if the Lord appears before us in the form of material energy, it is quite possible for Him to convert this material energy into spiritual energy. Since the source of the energies is one and the same, the energies can be utilized according to the will of their source. For example, the Lord can appear in the *arcā-vigraha*—that is, in the form of Deities supposedly made of earth, stone, or wood. These forms, although engraved from wood, stone, or other matter, are not idols, as the iconoclasts contend.

In our present state of imperfect material existence, we cannot see the Supreme Lord, due to imperfect vision. Yet those devotees who want to see Him by means of material vision are favored by the Lord, who appears in a so-called material form to accept His devotee's service. One should not think that such devotees, who are in the lowest stage of devotional service, are worshiping an idol. They are factually worshiping the Lord, who has agreed to appear before them in an approachable way. Nor is the *arcā* form fashioned according to the whims of the worshiper. It is eternally existent with all its paraphernalia. This can be actually felt by a sincere devotee, but not by an atheist.

In *Bhagavad-gītā* (4.11) the Lord indicates that He relates to His devotee in terms of the devotee's surrender. He reserves the right to expose Himself not to anyone and everyone but to those souls who are surrendered unto Him. Thus for the surrendered soul He is always within reach, whereas for the unsurrendered soul He is far, far away and cannot be approached.

In this connection the words *saguṇa* ("with qualities") and *nirguṇa* ("without qualities"), words occurring often in revealed scriptures, are very important. The word *saguṇa* does not imply that the Lord becomes subject to the laws of material nature when He appears, although He has perceivable qualities and appears in material form. For Him there is no difference between the material and spiritual energies, because He is the source of all energies. As the controller of all energies, He cannot at any time be under their influence, as we are. The material energy works according to His direction; therefore He can use that energy for His purpose without ever being influenced by any of the qualities of that energy. Nor does the Lord become a formless entity at any time, for ultimately He is the eternal form, the primeval Lord. His impersonal aspect, or Brahman effulgence, is but the glow of His personal rays, just as the sun's rays are the glow of the sun-god.

When the child-saint Prahlāda Mahārāja was in the presence of his atheist father, his father asked him, "Where is your God?" When Prahlāda replied that God resides everywhere, the father angrily asked whether his God was within one of the pillars of the palace, and the child said yes. The atheist immediately shattered the pillar in front of him to pieces, and the Lord instantly appeared as Nṛsiṁha, the half-man, half-lion incarnation, and killed the atheist king. Thus the Lord is within everything, and He creates everything by His different energies. Through His inconceivable powers He can appear at any place in order to favor His sincere devotee. Lord Nṛsiṁha appeared from within the pillar not by the order of the atheist king but by the wish of His devotee Prahlāda. An atheist cannot order the Lord to appear, but the Lord will appear anywhere and everywhere to show mercy to His devotee. *Bhagavad-gītā* (4.8) similarly states that the Lord appears to vanquish nonbelievers and protect believers. Of course, the Lord has sufficient energies and agents who can vanquish atheists, but it is pleasing for Him to personally favor a devotee. Therefore He descends as an incarnation. Actually, He descends only to favor His devotees and not for any other purpose.

In *Brahma-saṁhitā* it is said that Govinda, the primeval Lord, enters everything by His plenary portion. He enters the universe as well as all the atoms of the universe. He is outside of everything in His *virāṭ* form, and He is within everything as *antaryāmī*. As *antaryāmī* He witnesses everything that is going on, and He awards us the results of our actions as *karma-phala*. We ourselves may forget what we have done in previous lives, but because the Lord witnesses our actions, the results of our actions are always there, and we have to undergo the reactions nonetheless.

The fact is that there is nothing but God within and without. Everything is manifested by His different energies, just as heat and light emanate from fire, and in this way there is a oneness among the diverse energies. Although there is oneness, the Lord in His personal form still enjoys all that is enjoyable to the senses of the minuscule part-and-parcel living entities.

MANTRA SIX

यस्तु सर्वाणि भूतान्यात्मन्येवानुपश्यति ।
सर्वभूतेषु चात्मानं ततो न विजुगुप्सते ॥ ६ ॥

yas tu sarvāṇi bhūtāny
ātmany evānupaśyati
sarva-bhūteṣu cātmānaṁ
tato na vijugupsate

yaḥ—he who; *tu*—but; *sarvāṇi*—all; *bhūtāni*—living entities; *ātmani*—in relation with the Supreme Lord; *eva*—only; *anupaśyati*—observes in a systematic way; *sarva-bhūteṣu*—in every living being; *ca*—and; *ātmānam*—the Supersoul; *tataḥ*—thereafter; *na*—not; *vijugupsate*—hates anyone.

TRANSLATION

He who sees everything in relation to the Supreme Lord, who sees all entities as His parts and parcels, and who sees the Supreme Lord within everything, never hates anything nor any being.

PURPORT

This is a description of the *mahā-bhāgavata*, the great personality who sees everything in relation to the Supreme Personality of Godhead. There are three stages to realization of the Supreme Lord's presence. The *kaniṣṭha-adhikārī* is in the lower stage of realization. He goes to one place of worship, such as a temple, church, or mosque, according to his religious faith, and worships there according to scriptural injunctions. Such a devotee considers the Lord to be present at the place of worship and nowhere else. He cannot ascertain who is in what position in devotional service, nor can he tell who has realized the Supreme Lord. Such devotees follow the routine formulas and sometimes quarrel among themselves, considering one type of devotion better than another. These *kaniṣṭha-adhikārīs* are actually materialistic devotees who are simply trying to transcend the material boundaries in order to reach the spiritual plane.

Those who have attained the second stage of realization are called *madhyama-adhikārīs.* These devotees observe four principles, which are: (1) they see, first of all, the Supreme Lord, (2) they see next the devotees of the Lord, (3) they see the innocent, who have no knowledge of the Lord, and (4) they see the atheists, who have no faith in the Lord and who hate those in devotional service. The *madhyama-adhikārī* behaves differently according to circumstances. He adores the Lord, considering Him to be the object of love, and he makes friends with those who are in devotional service. He tries to awaken the dormant love of God in the hearts of the innocent, but he does not approach the atheists who deride the very name of the Lord.

In the third stage of realization is the *uttama-adhikārī,* who sees everything in relation to the Supreme Lord. Such a devotee does not discriminate between an atheist and a theist but sees everyone as part and parcel of God. He knows that there is no difference between a vastly learned *brāhmaṇa* and a dog in the street because both of them are of the Lord, although they are embodied differently according to the qualities of material nature. He sees that the *brāhmaṇa* particle of the Supreme Lord has not misused his little independence given him by the Lord and that the dog particle has misused his independence and is therefore punished by the laws of nature by being encaged in an ignorant form. Not considering the respective actions of the *brāhmaṇa* and the dog, the *uttama-adhikārī* tries to do good to both. Such a learned devotee is not misled by material bodies but is attracted by the spiritual spark within the respective entities.

Those who imitate an *uttama-adhikārī* by flaunting a sense of oneness or fellowship but who behave on the bodily platform are actually false philanthropists. The conception of universal brotherhood must be learned from an *uttama-adhikārī* and not from a foolish person who does not properly understand the individual soul and the Supersoul expansion of the Supreme Lord who dwells everywhere.

It is clearly mentioned in this sixth *mantra* that one should *observe*, or see. This means that one must follow the previous *ācārya*, the perfected teacher. *Anupaśyati* is the exact Sanskrit word used in this connection. *Paśyati* means "to observe." This does not mean that one should try to see things as he does with the naked eye. Due to material defects, the naked eye cannot see anything properly. One cannot see properly unless he has heard from a superior source, and the highest source is the Vedic wisdom, which is spoken by the Lord Himself. Vedic truths are coming in disciplic succession from the Lord to Brahmā, from Brahmā to Nārada, from Nārada to Vyāsa, and from Vyāsa to many other disciples. Formerly there was no need to record the messages of the *Vedas* because people in earlier ages were more intelligent and had sharper memories. They could follow instructions simply by hearing once from the mouth of a bona fide spiritual master.

At present there are many commentaries on the revealed scriptures, but most of them are not in the line of disciplic succession coming from Śrīla Vyāsadeva, who originally taught the Vedic wisdom. The final, most perfect and sublime work of Śrīla Vyāsadeva is *Śrīmad-Bhāgavatam*, which is the authorized commentary on the *Vedānta-sūtra*. There is also *Bhagavad-gītā*, which is spoken by the Lord Himself and which was recorded by Vyāsadeva. These are the most important revealed scriptures, and any commentary that contradicts the principles of the *Gītā* or *Śrīmad-Bhāgavatam* is unauthorized. There is complete agreement among the *Upaniṣads*, *Vedānta*, the *Vedas*, *Bhagavad-gītā*, and *Śrīmad-Bhāgavatam*, and no one should try to reach any conclusion about the *Vedas* without receiving instructions from members of Vyāsadeva's disciplic succession, or at least from those who believe in the Personality of Godhead and His diverse energies.

According to *Bhagavad-gītā* (6.9), only one who is already on the liberated platform can become an *uttama-adhikārī* devotee and see every living being as his own brother. This vision cannot be had by politicians, who are always after some material gain. When one imitates the symptoms of an *uttama-adhikārī*, he may serve his outward body for the purpose of fame or material reward, but he does not serve the spirit soul. Such an imitator can have no information of the spiritual world. The *uttama-adhikārī* sees the living entity's spirit soul and serves him as spirit. Thus the material aspect is automatically served.

MANTRA SEVEN

यस्मिन् सर्वाणि भूतान्यात्मैवाभूद् विजानतः ।
तत्र को मोहः कः शोक एकत्वमनुपश्यतः ॥ ७ ॥

yasmin sarvāṇi bhūtāny
ātmaivābhūd vijānataḥ
tatra ko mohaḥ kaḥ śoka
ekatvam anupaśyataḥ

yasmin—in the situation; *sarvāṇi*—all; *bhūtāni*—living entities; *ātmā*—the spiritual spark; *eva*—only; *abhūt*—exist as; *vijānataḥ*—of one who knows; *tatra*—therein; *kaḥ*—what; *mohaḥ*—illusion; *kaḥ*—what; *śokaḥ*—anxiety; *ekatvam*—oneness in quality; *anupaśyataḥ*—of one who sees through authority, or one who sees constantly like that.

TRANSLATION

One who always sees all living entities as spiritual sparks, in quality one with the Lord, becomes a true knower of things. What, then, can be illusion or anxiety for him?

PURPORT

But for the *madhyama-adhikārī* and *uttama-adhikārī* discussed above, no one can correctly see the spiritual position of a living being. The living entities are qualitatively one with the Supreme Lord, just as the sparks of a fire are qualitatively one with the nature of fire. Yet sparks are not fire as far as quantity is concerned, for the quantity of heat and light present in the sparks is not equal to that in fire. The *mahā-bhāgavata*, the great devotee, sees oneness in the sense that he sees everything as the energy of the Supreme Lord. Since there is no difference between the energy and the energetic, there is the sense of oneness. Although heat and light, from the analytical point of view, are different from fire, there is no meaning to the word *fire* without heat and light. But in synthesis, heat, light, and fire are all the same.

The Sanskrit words *ekatvam anupaśyataḥ* indicate that one should see the unity of all living entities from the viewpoint of revealed scriptures. The individual sparks of the supreme whole possess almost eighty percent of the known qualities of the whole, but they are not quantitatively equal to the Supreme Lord. These qualities are present in minute quantity, for the living entity is but a minute part and parcel of the supreme whole. To use another simile, the quantity of salt present in a drop is never comparable to the quantity of salt present in the complete ocean, but the salt present in the drop is qualitatively equal in chemical composition to all the salt present in the ocean. If the individual living being were equal to the Supreme Lord both qualitatively and quantitatively, there would be no question of his being under the influence of material energy. In the previous *mantras* it has already been discussed that no living being—not even the powerful demigods—can surpass the Supreme Being in any respect; therefore *ekatvam* does not mean that a living being is equal in all respects to the Supreme Lord. It does, however, indicate that in a broader sense there is one interest, just as in a family the interest of all members is one, or in a nation the national interest is one, although there are many different individual citizens. The living entities are all parts and parcels of the same supreme family, and the interest of the Supreme Being and that of the parts and parcels is not different. Every living being is the son of the Supreme Being. As stated in *Bhagavad-gītā* (14.3–4), all living creatures throughout the universe—including birds, reptiles, ants, aquatics, trees, and so on—are emanations of the marginal potency of the Supreme Lord. Therefore all of them belong to the family of the Supreme Being. There is no clash of interest in spiritual life.

The spiritual entities are meant for enjoyment. By nature and constitution, every living being—including the Supreme Lord and each part and parcel—is meant for eternal enjoyment. The living beings who are encaged in the material tabernacle are constantly seeking enjoyment, but they are seeking it on the wrong platform. Apart from this material world, there is the spiritual platform, where the Supreme Being enjoys Himself with His innumerable associates. On that platform there is no trace of material qualities, and therefore that platform is called *nirguṇa.* On the *nirguṇa* platform there is never a clash over the object of enjoyment. Here in the material world there is always a clash between different individual beings, because here the proper center of enjoyment is missed. The real center of enjoyment is the Supreme Lord, who is the center of the sublime and spiritual *rāsa* dance. We are all meant to join Him and enjoy life with one transcendental interest and without any clash. That is the high platform of spiritual interest, and as soon as one realizes this perfect form of oneness, there can be no question of illusion or lamentation.

A godless civilization arises from *māyā,* or illusion, and the result of such a civilization is lamentation. A godless civilization, such as that sponsored by the modern politicians, is always full of anxieties; that is the law of nature. As stated in *Bhagavad-gītā* (7.14), no one but those who surrender at the lotus feet of the Supreme Lord can surpass the stringent laws of nature. Thus if we wish to get rid of all sorts of illusion and anxiety and create unity out of all diverse interests, we must bring God into all our activities.

The results of our activities must be used to serve the interest of the Lord, and not for any other purpose. Only by serving the Lord's interest can we perceive the *ātma-bhūta* interest mentioned herein. The *ātma-bhūta* interest mentioned in this *mantra* and the *brahma-bhūta* interest mentioned in *Bhagavad-gītā* (18.54) are one and the same. The supreme *ātmā*, or soul, is the Lord Himself, and the minute *ātmā* is the living entity. The supreme *ātmā*, or Paramātmā, alone maintains all the individual minute beings, for the Supreme Lord wants to derive pleasure out of their affection. The father extends himself through his children and maintains them in order to derive pleasure. If the children are obedient to the father's will, family affairs will run smoothly with one interest and a pleasing atmosphere. The same situation is transcendentally arranged in the absolute family of the Parabrahman, the supreme spirit.

The Parabrahman is as much a person as the individual entities. Neither the Lord nor the living entities are impersonal. Such transcendental personalities are full of transcendental bliss, knowledge, and eternal life. That is the real position of spiritual existence, and as soon as one is fully cognizant of this transcendental position, he at once surrenders unto the lotus feet of the Supreme Being, Śrī Kṛṣṇa. But such a *mahātmā*, great soul, is very rarely seen, because such transcendental realization is achieved only after many, many births (Bg. 7.19). Once attained, however, there is no longer any illusion or distress or the miseries of material existence or birth and death, which are all experienced in our present life. That is the information we receive from this *mantra* of *Śrī Īśopaniṣad.*

MANTRA EIGHT

स पर्यगाच्छुक्रमकायमव्रण-
मस्नाविरꣳ शुद्धमपापविद्धम् ।
कविर् मनीषी परिभूः स्वयम्भूर्
याथातथ्यतोऽर्थान् व्यदधाच्छाश्वतीभ्यः समाभ्यः ॥८॥

sa paryagāc chukram akāyam avraṇam
asnāviraṁ śuddham apāpa-viddham
kavir manīṣī paribhūḥ svayambhūr
yāthātathyato 'rthān vyadadhāc chāśvatībhyaḥ samābhyaḥ

saḥ—that person; *paryagāt*—must know in fact; *śukram*—the omnipotent; *akāyam*—unembodied; *avraṇam*—without reproach; *asnāviram*—without veins; *śuddham*—antiseptic; *apāpa-viddham*—prophylactic; *kaviḥ*—omniscient; *manīṣī*—philosopher; *paribhūḥ*—the greatest of all; *svayambhūḥ*—self-sufficient; *yāthātathyataḥ*—just in pursuance of; *arthān*—desirables; *vyadadhāt*—awards; *śāśvatībhyaḥ*—immemorial; *samābhyaḥ*—time.

TRANSLATION

Such a person must factually know the greatest of all, who is unembodied, omniscient, beyond reproach, without veins, pure, and uncontaminated, the self-sufficient philosopher, who has been fulfilling everyone's desires since time immemorial.

PURPORT

This description of the transcendental and eternal form of the Absolute Personality of Godhead indicates that the Supreme Lord is not formless. He has His own transcendental form, which is not at all similar to the forms of the mundane world. The forms of the living entities in this world are embodied in material nature, and they work like any material machine. The anatomy of a material body must have a mechanical construction with veins and so forth, but the transcendental body of the Supreme Lord has nothing like veins. It is clearly stated here that He is unembodied, which means that there is no difference between His body and soul. Nor does He accept a body according to the law of nature, as we do. In the material conception of bodily life, the soul is different from the gross embodiment and subtle mind. However, the Supreme Lord is apart from any such compartmentalized arrangement. There is no difference between His body and mind. He is the complete whole, and His mind, body, and He Himself are all one and the same.

In *Brahma-saṁhitā* there is a similar description of the Supreme Lord. He is described there as *sac-cid-ānanda-vigraha,* which means that He is the eternal form fully representing transcendental existence, knowledge, and bliss. The Vedic literatures clearly state that He has a completely different kind of body; thus He is sometimes described as formless. This formlessness means that He has no form like ours and that He is devoid of a form which we can perceive. In *Brahma-saṁhitā* it is further stated that the Lord can do anything and everything with any one of the parts of His body. It is said there that with each and every one of the parts of His body, He can do the work of the other senses. This means that the Lord can walk with His hands, accept things with His legs, see with His hands and feet, eat with

His eyes, etc. In the *śruti-mantras* it is also said that although the Lord has no hands and legs like us, He has a different type of hands and legs, by which He can accept all that we offer Him and run faster than anyone. These points are confirmed in this eighth *mantra* through the use of words like *śukram* ("omnipotent").

The Lord's worshipable form (*arcā-vigraha*), which is installed in temples by authorized *ācāryas* who have realized the Lord in terms of Mantra Seven, is also nondifferent from the original form of the Lord. The Lord's original form is that of Śrī Kṛṣṇa, and Śrī Kṛṣṇa expands Himself into an unlimited number of forms like Baladeva, Rāma, Nṛsiṁha, Varāha, etc. All of these forms are one and the same Personality of Godhead.

Similarly, the *arcā-vigraha* that is worshiped in temples is also an expanded form of the Lord. By worshiping the *arcā-vigraha*, one can at once approach the Lord, who accepts the service of a devotee by His omnipotent energy. The *arcā-vigraha* of the Lord descends upon the request of the *ācāryas*, the holy teachers, and works exactly in the original way of the Lord by virtue of the Lord's omnipotent energy. Foolish people who have no knowledge of *Śrī Īśopaniṣad* or of any of the other *śruti-mantras* consider the *arcā-vigraha*, which is worshiped by pure devotees, to be made of material elements. This form may be seen as material by the imperfect eyes of foolish people or *kaniṣṭha-adhikārīs*, but such people do not know that the Lord, being omnipotent and omniscient, can transform matter into spirit and spirit into matter as He desires.

In *Bhagavad-gītā* (9.11–12) the Lord regrets the fallen condition of men with little knowledge who regard the body of the Lord as material just because the Lord descends like a man into this world. Such poorly informed persons do not know the omnipotence of the Lord. Thus the Lord does not manifest Himself in full to the mental speculators. He can be appreciated only in proportion to one's surrender to Him. The fallen condition of the living entities is due entirely to forgetfulness of their relationship with God.

In this *mantra*, as well as in many other Vedic *mantras*, it is clearly stated that the Lord has been supplying goods to the living entity from time immemorial. The living being desires something, and the Lord supplies the object of that desire in proportion to one's qualification. If a man wants to be a high court judge, he must not only acquire the necessary qualifications, but he must also acquire the consent of the authority who can award the title of high court judge. The qualifications in themselves are not sufficient in order for one to occupy the post. The post itself must be awarded by some superior authority. Similarly, the Lord awards enjoyment to living entities in proportion to their qualifications. In other words, they are awarded according to the law of *karma*. The qualifications in themselves are not sufficient to enable one to receive awards. The mercy of the Lord is also required.

Ordinarily the living being does not know what to ask from the Lord or which post to seek. When the living being comes to know his constitutional position, however, he asks to be accepted into the transcendental association of the Lord in order to render transcendental loving service unto Him. Unfortunately, living beings under the influence of material nature ask for many other things, and their mentality is described in *Bhagavad-gītā* (2.41) as divided or splayed intelligence. Spiritual intelligence is one, but mundane intelligence is diverse. In *Śrīmad-Bhāgavatam* it is stated that those who are captivated by the temporary beauties of the external energy forget the real aim of life, which is to go back to Godhead. Forgetting this, one tries to adjust things by various plans and programs, but this is like chewing that which has already been chewed. Nonetheless, the Lord is so kind that He allows the forgetful living entity to continue in this way without interference. If a living being wants to go to hell, the Lord allows him to do so without interference, and if he wants to go back home, back to Godhead, the Lord helps him.

God is described here as *paribhūḥ*, the greatest of all. No one is greater than or equal to Him. Other living beings are described here as beggars who ask goods from the Lord. The Lord supplies the things desired by the living entities. If the entities were equal to the Lord in potency, or if they were omnipotent or omniscient, there would be no question of their begging from the Lord, even for so-called liberation. Real liberation means going back to Godhead. Liberation as conceived by an impersonalist is a myth, and begging for sense gratification has to continue eternally unless the beggar comes to his spiritual senses and realizes his constitutional position.

Only the Supreme Lord is self-sufficient. When Lord Kṛṣṇa appeared on earth five thousand years ago, He displayed His full manifestation as the Personality of Godhead through His various activities. In His childhood He killed many powerful demons, and there was no question of His having acquired such power through any extraneous endeavor. He lifted Govardhana Hill without even practicing weight lifting. He danced with the *gopīs* without social restriction and without reproach. Although the *gopīs* approached Him with feelings of amorous love, the relationship between the *gopīs* and Lord Kṛṣṇa has been worshiped even by Lord Caitanya, who was a strict *sannyāsī* and rigid follower of disciplinary regulations. *Śrī Īśopaniṣad* also describes the Lord as *śuddham* ("antiseptic") and *apāpa-viddham* ("prophylactic"), or pure and uncontaminated. He is antiseptic in the sense that even an impure thing can become purified just by touching Him. The word *prophylactic* refers to the power of His association. As mentioned in *Bhagavad-gītā* (9.30–31), a devotee may appear to be *sudurācāra*, not well behaved, in the beginning, but he should be accepted as pure because he is on the right path. This is due to the prophylactic nature of the Lord's association. The Lord is also *apāpa-viddham*, because sin cannot touch Him. Even if He acts in a way which appears to be sinful, such actions are all-good, for there is no question of His being affected by sin. Because in all circumstances He is *śuddham*, most purified, He is often compared to the sun. The sun exacts moisture from many untouchable places on the earth, yet it remains pure. In fact, it purifies obnoxious things by virtue of its sterilizing powers. If the sun, which is a material object, is so powerful, then we can hardly begin to imagine the purity and strength of the all-powerful Lord.

MANTRA NINE

अन्धं तमः प्रविशन्ति येऽविद्यामुपासते ।
ततो भूय इव ते तमो य उ विद्यायाᳩ रताः ॥ ९ ॥

andhaṁ tamaḥ praviśanti
ye 'vidyām upāsate
tato bhūya iva te tamo
ya u vidyāyāṁ ratāḥ

andham—gross ignorance; *tamaḥ*—darkness; *praviśanti*—enter into; *ye*—those who; *avidyām*—nescience; *upāsate*—worship; *tataḥ*—than that; *bhūyaḥ*—still more; *iva*—like; *te*—they; *tamaḥ*—darkness; *ye*—those who; *u*—also; *vidyāyām*—in the culture of knowledge; *ratāḥ*—engaged.

TRANSLATION

Those who engage in the culture of nescient activities shall enter into the darkest region of ignorance. Worse still are those engaged in the culture of so-called knowledge.

PURPORT

This *mantra* offers a comparative study of *vidyā* and *avidyā*. *Avidyā*, or ignorance, is undoubtedly dangerous, but *vidyā*, or knowledge, is even more dangerous when mistaken or misguided. This *mantra* of *Śrī Īśopaniṣad* is even more applicable today than at any other time. Modern civilization has advanced considerably in the field of mass education, but the result is that people are more unhappy than ever before, because of the stress placed on material advancement to the exclusion of the most important part of life, the spiritual aspect.

As far as *vidyā* is concerned, the first *mantra* has explained very clearly that the Supreme Lord is the proprietor of everything and that forgetfulness of this fact is called ignorance. The more a man forgets this fact of life, the more he is in darkness. In view of this, a godless civilization directed toward the so-called advancement of education is more dangerous than a civilization in which the masses of people are less materially advanced.

Of the different classes of men—*karmīs*, *jñānīs*, and *yogīs*—the *karmīs* are those who are engaged in the activities of sense gratification. Almost 99.9 percent of the people in modern civilization are engaged in the activities of sense gratification under the flags of industrialism, economic development, altruism, political activism, and so on. Yet all these activities are more or less based on satisfaction of the senses to the exclusion of the kind of God consciousness described in the first *mantra*.

In the language of *Bhagavad-gītā* (7.15), people who are engaged in gross sense gratification are *mūḍhas*—asses. The ass is a symbol of stupidity. Those who simply engage in the profitless pursuit of sense gratification are worshiping *avidyā*, according to *Śrī Īśopaniṣad*. Those who play the role of helping this sort of civilization in the name of educational advancement are actually doing more harm than those who are on the platform of gross sense gratification. Advancement of learning by a godless people is as dangerous as a valuable jewel on the hood of a cobra. A cobra decorated with a valuable jewel is more dangerous than one not decorated. In *Hari-bhakti-sudhodaya* the advancement of education by a godless people is compared to decorations on a dead body. In India, as in many other countries, some people follow the custom of leading a procession with a decorated dead body for the pleasure of the lamenting relatives. In the same sense, modern civilization is a patchwork of activities meant to cover the perpetual miseries of material existence. Such activities are aimed toward sense gratification, but above the senses is the mind, and above the mind is the intelligence, and above the intelligence there is the soul. Thus the aim of real education should be self-realization, realization of the spiritual values of the soul. Any education that does not lead to such realization must be considered *avidyā*, or nescience. By the culture of such nescience, one goes down to the darkest region of ignorance.

According to the *Vedas*, mistaken mundane educators are known as (1) *veda-vāda-rata*, (2) *māyayāpahṛta-jñāna*, (3) *āsuraṁ bhāvam āśrita*, and (4) *narādhama*. Those who are *veda-vāda-rata* pose themselves as very learned in Vedic literature, but unfortunately they are completely diverted from the purpose of the *Vedas*. In *Bhagavad-gītā* (15.18–20) it is said that the Vedic goal is to know the Personality of Godhead, but these *veda-vāda-rata* men are not at all interested in the Personality of Godhead. On the contrary, they are fascinated by such fruitive results as the attainment of heaven, etc.

As stated in Mantra One, we should know that the Personality of Godhead is the proprietor of everything and that we must be satisfied with our allotted portions of the necessities of life. The purpose of all Vedic literature is to awaken this God consciousness in the forgetful living being, and this same purpose is presented in various ways in the different scriptures of the world for the understanding of a foolish mankind. Thus the ultimate purpose of all religions is to bring one back to Godhead.

But the *veda-vāda-rata* people, instead of realizing the purport of the *Vedas*, take it for granted that side issues such as the attainment of heavenly pleasure for sense gratification—the lust for which causes their material bondage in the first place—are the ultimate end of the *Vedas*. Such people misguide others by misinterpreting Vedic literature. Sometimes they even condemn the *Purāṇas*, which are authentic Vedic explanations for laymen. The *veda-vāda-ratas* give their own explanations of the *Vedas*, neglecting the authority of great teachers (*ācāryas*). They also tend to raise some unscrupulous person from among themselves and flaunt him as the leading exponent of Vedic knowledge. Such men are especially condemned in this *mantra* by the very appropriate Sanskrit word *vidyā-rata*. *Vidyā* means "*veda*," because the *Veda* is the origin of knowledge, and *rata* means "engaged." *Vidyā-rata* thus means "engaged in the study of the *Vedas*." The so-called *vidyā-ratas* are condemned herein because they do not know the actual purpose of the *Vedas*, due to their disobeying the *ācāryas*. Such *veda-vāda-ratas* are accustomed to finding meanings in every word of the *Vedas* to suit their own purposes. They do not know that Vedic literature is not a collection of ordinary books and cannot be understood but through the chain of disciplic succession.

One must approach a bona fide spiritual master in order to understand the transcendental message of the *Vedas*. That is the direction of *Kaṭha Upaniṣad*. These *veda-vāda-rata* people, however, have their own *ācārya*, who is not in the chain of transcendental succession. Thus they progress into the darkest region of ignorance by misinterpreting Vedic literature. They even fall further into ignorance than those who have no knowledge of the *Vedas* at all.

The *māyayāpahṛta-jñāna* class of men are self-made "gods." Such men think that they themselves are God and that there is no need to worship any other God. They will agree to worship an ordinary man if he happens to be rich, but they will never worship the Personality of Godhead. Such men, unable to recognize their own foolishness, never consider how it is that God can be entrapped by illusion. If God were ever entrapped by illusion, illusion would be more powerful than God. Such men say that God is all-powerful, but they do not consider that if He is all-powerful there is no possibility of His being overpowered by illusion. These self-made gods cannot answer all these questions very clearly; they are simply satisfied to have become God themselves.

MANTRA TEN

अन्यदेवाहुर्विद्ययान्यदाहुरविद्यया ।
इति शुश्रुम धीराणां ये नस्तद् विचचक्षिरे ॥ १० ॥

anyad evāhur vidyayā
anyad āhur avidyayā
iti śuśruma dhīrāṇāṁ
ye nas tad vicacakṣire

anyat—different; *eva*—certainly; *āhuḥ*—said; *vidyayā*—by culture of knowledge; *anyat*—different; *āhuḥ*—said; *avidyayā*—by culture of nescience; *iti*—thus; *śuśruma*—I heard; *dhīrāṇām*—from the sober; *ye*—who; *naḥ*—to us; *tat*—that; *vicacakṣire*—explained.

TRANSLATION

The wise have explained that one result is derived from the culture of knowledge and that a different result is obtained from the culture of nescience.

PURPORT

As advised in the Thirteenth Chapter of *Bhagavad-gītā* (13.8–12), one should culture knowledge in the following way.

1. One should himself become a perfect gentleman and learn to give proper respect to others.

2. One should not pose himself as a religionist simply for name and fame.

3. One should not become a source of anxiety to others by the actions of his body, by the thoughts of his mind, or by his words.

4. One should learn forbearance even in the face of provocation from others.

5. One should learn to avoid duplicity in his dealings with others.

6. One should search out a bona fide spiritual master who can lead him gradually to the stage of spiritual realization, and one must submit himself to such a spiritual master, render him service, and ask relevant questions.

7. In order to approach the platform of self-realization, one must follow the regulative principles enjoined in the revealed scriptures.

8. One must be fixed in the tenets of the revealed scriptures.

9. One should completely refrain from practices that are detrimental to the interest of self-realization.

10. One should not accept more than he requires for the maintenance of the body.

11. One should not falsely identify himself with the gross material body or consider those who are related to his body to be his own.

12. One should always remember that as long as he has a material body he must face the miseries of repeated birth, old age, disease, and death. There is no use in making plans to get rid of these miseries of the material body. The best course is to find out the means by which one may regain his spiritual identity.

13. One should not be attached to more than the necessi-

ties of life required for spiritual advancement.

14. One should not be more attached to wife, children, and home than the revealed scriptures ordain.

15. One should not be happy or distressed over desirables and undesirables created by the mind.

16. One should become an unalloyed devotee of the Personality of Godhead, Śrī Kṛṣṇa, and serve Him with rapt attention.

17. One should develop a liking for residence in a secluded place with a calm and quiet atmosphere favorable for spiritual culture, and one should avoid congested places where nondevotees congregate.

18. One should become a scientist or philosopher and conduct research into spiritual knowledge, recognizing that spiritual knowledge is permanent whereas material knowledge ends with the death of the body.

These eighteen items combine to form a gradual process by which real knowledge can be developed. But for these, all other methods are considered to be in the category of nescience. Śrīla Bhaktivinoda Ṭhākura, a great *ācārya*, maintained that all forms of material knowledge are merely external features of the illusory energy and that by culturing them one becomes no better than an ass. This same principle is found in *Śrī Īśopaniṣad.* By advancement of material knowledge, modern man is simply being converted into an ass. Some materialistic politicians in spiritual guise decry the present system of civilization as satanic, but unfortunately they do not care about the culture of real knowledge as it is described in *Bhagavad-gītā.* Thus they cannot change the satanic situation.

In the modern setup, even a boy thinks himself self-sufficient and pays no respect to elderly men. Due to the wrong type of education being imparted in our universities, boys all over the world have caused elderly people headaches. Thus *Śrī Īśopaniṣad* very strongly warns that the culture of nescience is different from that of knowledge. The universities are, so to speak, centers of nescience only; consequently scientists are busy discovering lethal weapons to wipe out the existence of other countries. University students today are not given instructions in the regulative principles of *brahmacarya* nor in the spiritual process of life. Nor do they have any faith in any scriptural injunctions. Religious principles are taught for the sake of name and fame only and not for the sake of practical action. Thus there is animosity not only in social and political fields but in the field of religion as well.

Nationalism and chauvinism have developed in different parts of the world due to the cultivation of nescience by the general people. No one considers that this tiny earth is just a lump of matter floating in immeasurable space along with many other lumps. In comparison to the vastness of space, these material lumps are like dust particles in air. Because God has kindly made these lumps of matter complete in themselves, they are perfectly equipped with all necessities for floating in space. The drivers of our spaceships may be very proud of their achievements, but they do not consider the supreme driver of these greater, more gigantic spaceships called planets.

There are innumerable suns and innumerable planetary systems also. As the infinitesimal parts and parcels of the Supreme Lord, we small creatures are trying to dominate these unlimited planets. Thus we take repeated birth and death and are generally frustrated by old age and disease. The span of human life is scheduled for about a hundred years, although it is gradually decreasing to twenty or thirty years. Thanks to the culture of nescience, befooled men have created their own nations within these planets in order to more effectively grasp sense enjoyment for these few years. Such foolish people are drawing up various plans to render national demarcations as perfect as possible. This is ultimately ridiculous. For this purpose each and every nation has become a source of anxiety for others. More than fifty percent of a nation's energy is devoted to defense measures and thus spoiled. No one cares for the cultivation of knowledge, and yet people are falsely proud of being advanced in both material and spiritual knowledge.

Śrī Īśopaniṣad warns us of this faulty type of education, and *Bhagavad-gītā* gives instructions as to the development of real knowledge. In this *mantra* there is a hint that the instructions of *vidyā* (knowledge) must be acquired from a *dhīra.* A *dhīra* is one who is not disturbed by material illusion. No one can be undisturbed unless he is perfectly spiritually realized, at which time one neither hankers nor laments for anything. A *dhīra* realizes that the material body and mind, which he has acquired by chance through material association, are but foreign elements; therefore he simply makes the best use of a bad bargain.

The material body and mind are bad bargains for the spiritual living entity. The living entity has actual functions in the living spiritual world, but this material world is dead. As long as the living spiritual sparks manipulate the dead lumps of matter, the dead world appears to be a living world. Actually it is the living souls, the parts and parcels of the supreme living being, who move the world. The *dhīras* are those who have come to know all these facts by hearing of them from superior authorities. The *dhīras* realize this knowledge by following the regulative principles.

To follow the regulative principles, one must take shelter of a bona fide spiritual master. The transcendental message and regulative principles come down from the spiritual master to the disciple. Such knowledge does not come in the hazardous way of nescient education. One can become a *dhīra* only by submissively hearing the messages of the Personality of Godhead. The perfect disciple must be like Arjuna, and the spiritual master must be as good as the Lord Himself. This is the process of learning *vidyā* (knowledge) from the *dhīra*, the undisturbed.

An *adhīra* (one who has not undergone the training of a *dhīra*) cannot be an instructive leader. Modern politicians who pose themselves as *dhīras* are actually *adhīras*, and one cannot expect perfect knowledge from them. They are simply busy seeing to their own remuneration in dollars and cents. How then can they lead the mass of people to the right path of self-realization? Thus one must hear submissively from the *dhīra* in order to attain actual education.

MANTRA ELEVEN

विद्यां चाविद्यां च यस्तद् वेदोभयꣳ सह ।
अविद्यया मृत्युं तीर्त्वा विद्ययामृतमश्नुते ॥ ११ ॥

vidyāṁ cāvidyāṁ ca yas
tad vedobhayaṁ saha
avidyayā mṛtyuṁ tīrtvā
vidyayāmṛtam aśnute

vidyām—knowledge in fact; *ca*—and; *avidyām*—nescience; *ca*—and; *yaḥ*—a person who; *tat*—that; *veda*—knows; *ubhayam*—both; *saha*—simultaneously; *avidyayā*—by culture of nescience; *mṛtyum*—repeated death; *tīrtvā*—transcending; *vidyayā*—by culture of knowledge; *amṛtam*—deathlessness; *aśnute*—enjoys.

TRANSLATION

Only one who can learn the process of nescience and that of transcendental knowledge side by side can transcend the influence of repeated birth and death and enjoy the full blessing of immortality.

PURPORT

Since the creation of the material world, everyone has been trying to attain a permanent life, but the law of nature is so cruel that no one has been able to avoid the hand of death. It is an actual fact that no one wants to die. Nor does anyone want to become old or diseased. The law of nature, however, does not allot anyone immunity from death, old age, or disease. Nor has the advancement of material knowledge solved these problems. Material science can discover the nuclear bomb to accelerate the process of death, but it cannot discover anything that can protect man from the cruel hands of disease, old age, and death.

From the *Purāṇas* we learn of the activities of Hiraṇyakaśipu, a king who was very much advanced materially. Wanting to conquer death by his material acquisitions and the strength of his nescience, he underwent a type of meditation so severe that the inhabitants of all the planetary systems became disturbed by his mystic powers. He forced the creator of the universe, the demigod Brahmā, to come down to him. He then asked Brahmā for the benediction of *amara*, by which one does not die. Brahmā said that he could not award the benediction because even he, the material creator who rules all planets, is not *amara*. As confirmed in *Bhagavad-gītā* (8.17), Brahmā lives a long time, but that does not mean he does not have to die.

Hiraṇya means "gold," and *kaśipu* means "soft bed." This gentleman was interested in these two things—money and women—and he wanted to enjoy them by becoming immortal. He asked Brahmā many questions indirectly, in hopes of fulfilling his desire to become an *amara*. Since Brahmā told him that he could not grant the gift of immortality, Hiraṇyakaśipu requested that he not be killed by any man, animal, god, or any other living being within the categories of the 8,400,000 species. He also requested that he not die on land, in the air, or in the water, or by any weapon whatsoever. In this way Hiraṇyakaśipu foolishly thought that these guarantees would save him from death.

Ultimately, however, although Brahmā granted him all these benedictions, he was killed by the Personality of Godhead in the form of Nṛsiṁha, a half-lion, half-man, and no weapon was used to kill him, for he was killed by the nails of the Lord. Nor was he killed on the land, in the air, or in the water, for he was killed on the lap of that wonderful living being who was beyond his conception.

The whole point here is that even Hiraṇyakaśipu, the most powerful of materialists, could not become deathless by his various plans. What, then, can be accomplished by the tiny Hiraṇyakaśipus of today, whose plans are throttled from moment to moment?

Śrī Īśopaniṣad instructs us not to make onesided attempts to win the struggle for existence. Everyone is struggling hard for existence, but the laws of material nature are so hard and fast that they do not allow anyone to surpass them. In order to attain a permanent life, one must be prepared to go back to Godhead.

The process by which one goes back to Godhead is a different branch of knowledge, and it has to be learned from revealed Vedic scriptures such as the *Upaniṣads, Vedānta-sūtra, Bhagavad-gītā, Śrīmad-Bhāgavatam,* etc. To become happy in this life and attain a permanent blissful life after leaving this material body, one must take to this sacred literature and obtain transcendental knowledge. The conditioned living being has forgotten his eternal relationship with God, and he has mistakenly accepted the temporary place of birth as all in all. The Lord has kindly delivered the above-mentioned scriptures in India and other scriptures in other countries to remind the forgetful human being that his home is not here in this material world. The living being is a spiritual entity, and he can only be happy by returning to his spiritual home.

The Personality of Godhead sends His bona fide servants

from His kingdom to propagate this message by which one can return to Godhead, and sometimes the Lord comes Himself to do this work. Since all living beings are His beloved sons, His parts and parcels, God is more sorry than we ourselves to see the sufferings which we are constantly undergoing in this material condition. The miseries of this material world serve to indirectly remind us of our incompatibility with dead matter. Intelligent living entities generally take note of these reminders and engage themselves in the culture of *vidyā*, or transcendental knowledge. Human life is the best opportunity for the culture of spiritual knowledge, and a human being who does not take advantage of this opportunity is called a *narādhama*, the lowest of human beings.

The path of *avidyā*, or advancement of material knowledge for sense gratification, is the path of repeated birth and death. As he exists spiritually, the living entity has no birth or death. Birth and death apply to the outward covering of the spirit soul, the body. Death is compared to the taking off, and birth to the putting on, of outward garments. Foolish human beings who are grossly absorbed in the culture of *avidyā*, nescience, do not mind this cruel process. Being enamored by the beauty of illusory energy, they undergo the same things repeatedly and do not learn any lessons from the laws of nature.

The culture of *vidyā*, or transcendental knowledge, is essential for the human being. Sense enjoyment in the diseased material condition must be restricted as far as possible. Unrestricted sense enjoyment in this bodily condition is the path of ignorance and death. The living entities are not without spiritual senses; every living being in his original, spiritual form has all the senses, which are now material, being covered by the body and mind. Activities of the material senses are perverted reflections of spiritual pastimes.

In its diseased condition, the spirit soul engages in material activities under the material covering. Real sense enjoyment is possible only when the disease of materialism is removed. In our real, spiritual form, free from all material contamination, pure enjoyment of the senses is possible. The aim of human life should not be perverted sense enjoyment; one should be eager to cure the material disease. Aggravation of the material disease is no sign of knowledge, but a sign of *avidyā,* ignorance. A fever must not be increased from 105 degrees to 107 degrees for good health, but should be reduced to the normal 98.6. That should be the aim of human life. The modern trend of material civilization is to increase the temperature of the feverish material condition, which has reached the point of 107 degrees in the form of atomic energy. Meanwhile, the foolish politicians are crying that at any moment the world may go to hell. That is the result of the advancement of material knowledge and neglect of the most important kind of life, the culture of spiritual knowledge. *Śrī Īśopaniṣad* herein warns that we must not follow this dangerous path, which leads to death. On the contrary, we must develop the culture of spiritual knowledge, so that we may become completely free from the cruel hands of death.

This does not mean that all activities for the maintenance of the body should be stopped. There is no question of stopping activities, just as there is no question of wiping out one's temperature altogether when trying to recover from a disease. "To make the best use of a bad bargain" is the appropriate expression. The culture of spiritual knowledge necessitates the help of this body and mind; therefore maintenance of the body and mind is required if we are to reach our goal. The normal temperature should be maintained at 98.6 degrees, and the great sages and saints of India have attempted to do this by a balanced program of spiritual and material knowledge. They never allow the misuse of human intelligence for diseased sense gratification.

Human activities diseased by a tendency toward sense gratification have been regulated in the *Vedas* under the principles of salvation. This system employs religion, economic development, sense gratification, and salvation, but at the present moment people have no interest in religion or salvation. They have only one aim in life—sense gratification—and in order to fulfill this end they make plans for economic development. Misguided men think that religion should be maintained because it contributes to economic development, which is required for sense gratification. Thus in order to guarantee further sense gratification after death, in heaven, there is some system of religious observance. This, however, is not the purpose of salvation. The path of religion is actually for self-realization, and economic development is required just to maintain the body in a sound, healthy condition. A man should lead a healthy life with a sound mind just to realize *vidyā*, true knowledge, which is the aim of human life. This life is not meant for working like an ass or for culturing *avidyā* for sense gratification.

The path of *vidyā* is most perfectly presented in *Śrīmad-Bhāgavatam*, which directs a human being to utilize his life to inquire into the Absolute Truth. The Absolute Truth is realized step by step as Brahman, Paramātmā, and finally Bhagavān, the Personality of Godhead. The Absolute Truth is realized by the broadminded man who has attained knowledge and detachment by following the eighteen principles of *Bhagavad-gītā* described in the purport to Mantra Ten. The central purpose of these eighteen principles is the attainment of transcendental devotional service to the Personality of Godhead. Therefore all classes of men are encouraged to learn the art of devotional service to the Lord. The guaranteed path to the aim of *vidyā* is described by Śrī Rūpa Gosvāmī in his *Bhakti-rasāmṛta-sindhu,* which we have presented in English as *The Nectar of Devotion.* The culture of *vidyā* is summarized by the *Śrīmad-Bhāgavatam* (1.2.14) in the following words:

tasmād ekena manasā
bhagavān sātvatāṁ patiḥ
śrotavyaḥ kīrtitavyaś ca
dhyeyaḥ pūjyaś ca nityadā

"Therefore devotees should constantly hear about, glorify, remember, and worship the Personality of Godhead [Bhagavān], who is their protector."

Unless religion, economic development, and sense gratification aim toward the attainment of devotional service to the Lord, they are all simply different forms of nescience, as *Śrī Īśopaniṣad* indicates in the following *mantras.* To culture *vidyā* in this age, one must always hear, chant, and worship with concentrated attention aimed at the Personality of Godhead, who is the Lord of the transcendentalists.

MANTRA TWELVE

**अन्धं तमः प्रविशन्ति येऽसम्भूतिमुपासते ।
ततो भूय इव ते तमो य उ सम्भूत्यां रताः ॥ १२ ॥**

andhaṁ tamaḥ praviśanti
ye 'sambhūtim upāsate
tato bhūya iva te tamo
ya u sambhūtyāṁ ratāḥ

andham—ignorance; *tamaḥ*—darkness; *praviśanti*—enter into; *ye*—those who; *asambhūtim*—demigods; *upāsate*—worship; *tataḥ*—than that; *bhūyaḥ*—still more; *iva*—like that; *te*—those; *tamaḥ*—darkness; *ye*—who; *u*—also; *sambhūtyām*—in the Absolute; *ratāḥ*—engaged.

TRANSLATION

Those who are engaged in the worship of demigods enter into the darkest region of ignorance, and still more so do the worshipers of the impersonal Absolute.

PURPORT

The Sanskrit word *asambhūti* refers to those who have no independent existence. *Sambhūti* is the Absolute Personality of Godhead, who is absolutely independent of everything. In *Bhagavad-gītā* (10.2), the Absolute Personality of Godhead, Śrī Kṛṣṇa, states,

na me viduḥ sura-gaṇāḥ
prabhavaṁ na maharṣayaḥ
aham ādir hi devānāṁ
maharṣīṇāṁ ca sarvaśaḥ

"Neither the hosts of demigods nor the great sages know My origin, for in every respect, I am the source of the demigods and the sages." Thus Kṛṣṇa is the origin of the powers delegated to demigods, great sages, and mystics. Although they are endowed with great powers, it is very difficult for them to know how Kṛṣṇa Himself appears by His own internal potency in the form of a man.

All philosophers and great *ṛṣis*, or mystics, try to distinguish the Absolute from the relative by their tiny brain power. This can only help them reach the point of negating relativity without realizing any positive trace of the Absolute. Definition of the Absolute by negation is not complete. Such negative definitions lead one to create a concept of his own; thus one imagines that the Absolute must be formless and without qualities. Negative qualities are simply the reversals of positive qualities and are therefore also relative. By conceiving of the Absolute in this way, one can at the utmost reach the impersonal effulgence of God, known as Brahman, but he cannot make further progress to Bhagavān, the Personality of Godhead.

Such mental speculators do not know that Kṛṣṇa is the Absolute Personality of Godhead, that the impersonal Brahman is the glaring effulgence of His transcendental body, and that Paramātmā, the Supersoul, is His all-pervading representation. Nor do they know that Kṛṣṇa has His eternal form with its transcendental qualities of eternal bliss and knowledge. The dependent demigods and great sages imperfectly consider Him to be a powerful demigod, and they consider the Brahman effulgence to be the Absolute Truth. Kṛṣṇa's devotees who surrender unto Him in unalloyed devotion, however, can know that He is the Absolute Person and that everything emanates from Him. Such devotees continuously render loving service unto Kṛṣṇa, the fountainhead of everything.

In *Bhagavad-gītā* (7.20) it is also said that only bewildered persons, driven by a strong desire for sense gratification, worship the demigods for the satisfaction of temporary problems. Temporary relief from certain difficulties by the greatness of some demigod is a solution sought only by the unintelligent. Since the living being is materially entangled, he has to be relieved from material bondage entirely, to attain permanent relief on the spiritual plane, where eternal bliss, life, and knowledge exist. It is also stated in *Bhagavad-gītā* (7.23) that the worshipers of the demigods can go to the planets of the demigods. The moon worshipers can go to the moon, the sun worshipers to the sun, etc. Modern scientists are now venturing to the moon with the help of rockets, but this is not really a new attempt. With their advanced consciousness, human beings are naturally inclined to travel in outer space and to reach other planets—either by spaceships, mystic powers, or demigod worship. In the Vedic scriptures it is said that one can reach other planets by any one of these three ways, but the most common way is by worshiping the demigod presiding over that particular planet. However, all planets in the material universe are temporary residences; the only permanent planets are the Vaikuṇṭhalokas. These are found in the spiritual sky, and the Personality of Godhead Himself dominates them. As stated in *Bhagavad-gītā* (8.16),

ābrahma-bhuvanāl lokāḥ
punar āvartino 'rjuna
mām upetya tu kaunteya
punar janma na vidyate

"From the highest planet in the material world down to the lowest, all are places of misery wherein repeated birth and death take place. But one who attains My abode, O son of Kuntī, never takes birth again."

Śrī Īśopaniṣad points out that one remains in the darkest region of the universe by hovering over the material planets by one means or another. The whole universe is covered by the gigantic material elements, just as a coconut is covered by a husk. Since its covering is airtight, the darkness within is dense, and therefore planets like the sun and the moon are required for illumination. Outside the universe is the vast and unlimited *brahmajyoti* expansion, which is filled with Vaikuṇṭhalokas. The highest planet in the *brahmajyoti* is the Kṛṣṇaloka, or Goloka Vṛndāvana, where the Supreme Personality of Godhead, Śrī Kṛṣṇa Himself, resides. Lord Śrī Kṛṣṇa never leaves this Kṛṣṇaloka. Although He dwells there with His eternal associates, He is omnipresent throughout the complete material and spiritual cosmic manifestations. This fact has already been explained in Mantra Four. The Lord is present everywhere, just like the sun, yet He is situated in one place, just as the sun is situated in its own undeviating orbit.

The problems of life cannot be solved simply by going to the moon. There are many pseudoworshipers who become religionists only for the sake of name and fame. Such pseudoreligionists do not wish to get out of this universe and reach the spiritual sky. They want only to maintain the status quo in the material world under the garb of worshiping the Lord. The atheists and impersonalists lead such foolish pseudoreligionists into the darkest regions by preaching the cult of atheism. The atheist directly denies the existence of the Supreme Personality of Godhead, and the impersonalists support the atheists by stressing the impersonal aspect of the Supreme Lord. Thus far we have not come across any *mantra* in *Śrī Īśopaniṣad* in which the Supreme Personality of Godhead is denied. It is said that He can run faster than anyone. Those who are running after other planets are certainly persons, and if the Lord can run faster than all of them, how can He be considered impersonal? The impersonal conception of the Supreme Lord is another form of ignorance, arising from an imperfect conception of the Absolute Truth.

The ignorant pseudoreligionists and the manufacturers of so-called incarnations who directly violate the Vedic injunctions are liable to enter into the darkest region of the universe because they mislead those who follow them. These impersonalists generally pose themselves as incarnations of God to the foolish who have no knowledge of Vedic wisdom. If such foolish men have any knowledge at all, it is more dangerous in their hands than ignorance itself. Such impersonalists do not even worship the demigods according to the scriptural recommendations. In the scriptures there are recommendations for worshiping demigods under certain circumstances, but at the same time these scriptures state that there is normally no need for this. In *Bhagavad-gītā* (7.23) it is clearly stated that the results derived from worshiping the demigods are not permanent. Since the entire material universe is not permanent, whatever is achieved within the darkness of material existence is also impermanent. The question is how to obtain real and permanent life.

The Lord states that as soon as one reaches Him by devotional service—which is the one and only way to approach the Personality of Godhead—one attains complete freedom from the bondage of birth and death. In other words, the path of salvation from the material clutches fully depends on the principles of knowledge and detachment. The pseudoreligionists have neither knowledge of nor detachment from material affairs, for most of them want to live in the golden shackles of material bondage under the shadow of altruistic and philanthropic activities and in the guise of religious principles. By a false display of religious sentiments, they present a show of devotional service while indulging in all sorts of immoral activities. In this way they pass as spiritual masters and devotees of God. Such violators of religious principles have no respect for the authoritative *ācāryas*, the holy teachers in the strict disciplic succession. To mislead the people in general, they themselves become so-called *ācāryas*, but they do not even follow the principles of the *ācāryas*.

These rogues are the most dangerous elements in human society. Because there is no religious government, they escape punishment by the law of the state. They cannot, however, escape the law of the Supreme, who has clearly declared in *Bhagavad-gītā* (16.19–20) that envious demons in the garb of religious propagandists shall be thrown into the darkest regions of hell. *Śrī Īśopaniṣad* confirms that these pseudoreligionists are heading toward the most obnoxious place in the universe after the completion of their spiritual-master business, which they conduct simply for sense gratification.

MANTRA THIRTEEN

अन्यदेवाहुः सम्भवादन्यदाहुरसम्भवात् ।
इति शुश्रुम धीराणां ये नस्तद्विचचक्षिरे ॥ १३ ॥

anyad evāhuḥ sambhavād
anyad āhur asambhavāt
iti śuśruma dhīrāṇāṁ
ye nas tad vicacakṣire

anyat—different; *eva*—certainly; *āhuḥ*—it is said; *sambhavāt*—by worshiping the Supreme Lord, the cause of all causes; *anyat*—different; *āhuḥ*—it is said; *asambhavāt*—by worshiping what is not the Supreme; *iti*—thus; *śuśruma*—I heard it; *dhīrāṇām*—from the undisturbed authorities; *ye*—who; *naḥ*—unto us; *tat*—about that subject matter; *vicacakṣire*—perfectly explained.

TRANSLATION

It is said that one result is obtained by worshiping the supreme cause of all causes and that another result is obtained by worshiping that which is not supreme. All this is heard from the undisturbed authorities who clearly explained it.

PURPORT

The system of hearing from undisturbed authorities is approved in this *mantra.* Unless one hears from a bona fide *ācārya,* who is never disturbed about the changes of the material world, one cannot have the real key to transcendental knowledge. The bona fide spiritual master, who has also heard the *śruti-mantras,* or Vedic knowledge, from his undisturbed *ācārya,* never manufactures or presents anything which is not mentioned in the Vedic literatures. In *Bhagavad-gītā* (9.25) it is clearly said that those who worship the Pitās, or forefathers, attain the planets of the forefathers. Similarly, the gross materialists who make plans to remain here again attain this world, and the devotees of the Lord, who worship none but Lord Kṛṣṇa, the supreme cause of all causes, reach Him in His abode in the spiritual sky.

Here also in *Śrī Īśopaniṣad* it is verified that different results are achieved by different modes of worship. If we worship the Supreme Lord, we will certainly reach Him in His eternal abode, and if we worship demigods like the sun-god and moon-god, we can reach their respective planets without a doubt. And if we wish to remain on this wretched planet with our planning commissions and our stopgap political adjustments, we can certainly do that also.

Nowhere in authentic scriptures is it said that one will ultimately reach the same goal by doing anything or worshiping anyone. Such foolish theories are offered by self-made masters, who have no connection with the *paramparā,* the bona fide system of disciplic succession. The bona fide spiritual master cannot say that all paths lead to the same goal and that anyone can attain this goal by his own mode of worship of the demigods or of the Supreme or whatever. For a common man it is very easy to understand that a person can reach his destination only when he has purchased a ticket for that destination. A person who has purchased a ticket for Calcutta can reach Calcutta, but not Bombay. However, temporary so-called masters say that any and all tickets can take one to the supreme goal. Such mundane and compromising offers attract many foolish creatures, who become puffed up with their manufactured methods of spiritual realization. The Vedic instructions, however, do not uphold them. Unless one has received knowledge from the bona fide spiritual master who is in the recognized line of disciplic succession, he cannot have the real thing as it is. Kṛṣṇa tells Arjuna in *Bhagavad-gītā* (4.2),

evaṁ paramparā-prāptam
imaṁ rājarṣayo viduḥ
sa kāleneha mahatā
yogo naṣṭaḥ parantapa

"This supreme science was thus received through the chain of disciplic succession, and the saintly kings understood it in that way. But in course of time the succession was broken, and therefore the science as it is appears to be lost."

When Lord Śrī Kṛṣṇa was present on this earth, the *bhakti-yoga* principles, which had been defined in *Bhagavad-gītā*, had become distorted; therefore the Lord had to reestablish the disciplic system, beginning with Arjuna, who was the most confidential friend and devotee of the Lord. The Lord clearly told Arjuna (Bg. 4.3) that it was because he was His devotee and friend that the principles of *Bhagavad-gītā* were understandable to him. In other words, no one can understand the *Gītā* who is not a devotee and friend of the Lord. This also means that only one who follows the path of Arjuna can understand *Bhagavad-gītā*.

At the present moment there are many interpreters and

translators of this sublime dialogue who really have no knowledge of Lord Kṛṣṇa's instructions to Arjuna. Such interpreters explain the verses of *Bhagavad-gītā* in their own way and postulate all sorts of rubbish in the name of scripture. Such interpreters believe neither in Śrī Kṛṣṇa nor in His eternal abode. How, then, can they explain *Bhagavad-gītā*?

The *Gītā* (7.20) clearly says that only those who have lost their sense worship the demigods. Kṛṣṇa ultimately advises that one give up all other ways and modes of worship and fully surrender unto Him only (Bg. 18.66). Only those who are cleansed of all sinful reactions can have such unflinching faith in the Supreme Lord. Others will continue hovering on the material platform with their paltry ways of worship and thus will be misled from the real path under the false impression that all paths lead to the same goal.

In this *mantra* the word *sambhavāt* ("by worship of the supreme cause") is very significant. Lord Kṛṣṇa is the original Personality of Godhead, and everything that exists has emanated from Him. In *Bhagavad-gītā* (10.8) the Lord explains that He is the creator of everyone, including Brahmā, Viṣṇu, and Śiva. Because these three principal deities of the material world are created by the Lord, the Lord is the creator of all that exists in the material and spiritual worlds. In the *Atharva Veda* it is similarly said that He who existed before the creation of Brahmā and who enlightened Brahmā with Vedic knowledge is Lord Śrī Kṛṣṇa. "The Supreme Person desired to create living entities, and thus Nārāyaṇa created all living beings. From Nārāyaṇa, Brahmā was born. Nārāyaṇa created all the Prajāpatis. Nārāyaṇa created Indra. Nārāyaṇa created the eight Vasus. Nārāyaṇa created the eleven Rudras. Nārāyaṇa created the twelve Ādityas." Since Nārāyaṇa is the plenary manifestation of Lord Kṛṣṇa, Nārāyaṇa and Kṛṣṇa are one and the same. There are also later readings which state that the same Supreme Lord is the son of Devakī. Śrī Kṛṣṇa's childhood with Devakī and Vasudeva and His identity with Nārāyaṇa have also been accepted and confirmed by Śrīpāda Śaṅkarācārya, even though Śaṅkara does not belong to the Vaiṣṇava, or personalist, cult. The *Atharva Veda* also states, "Only Nārāyaṇa existed in the beginning when neither Brahmā, nor Śiva, nor fire, nor water, nor stars, nor sun, nor moon existed. The Lord does not remain alone but creates as He desires." It is stated in the *Mokṣa-dharma*, "I created the Prajāpatis and the Rudras. They do not have complete knowledge of Me because they are covered by My illusory energy." It is also stated in *Varāha Purāṇa*, "Nārāyaṇa is the Supreme Personality of Godhead, and from Him the four-headed Brahmā was manifested, as well as Rudra, who later became omniscient."

Thus all Vedic literature confirms that Nārāyaṇa, or Kṛṣṇa, is the cause of all causes. In *Brahma-saṁhitā* also it is said that the Supreme Lord is Śrī Kṛṣṇa, Govinda, the delight of every living being and the primeval cause of all causes. The really learned person knows this from evidence given by the great sages and the *Vedas*. Thus the learned man decides to worship Lord Kṛṣṇa as all in all.

Persons are called *budha*, or really learned, when they fasten themselves to the worship of Kṛṣṇa only. This conviction is established when one hears the transcendental message from the undisturbed *ācārya* with faith and love. One who has no faith in or love for Lord Kṛṣṇa cannot be convinced of this simple truth. Those who are faithless are described in *Bhagavad-gītā* (9.11) as *mūḍhas*, fools or asses. It is said that the *mūḍhas* deride the Personality of Godhead because they do not have complete knowledge from the undisturbed *ācārya*. One who is disturbed by the whirlpool of material energy is not qualified to become an *ācārya*.

Before hearing *Bhagavad-gītā*, Arjuna was disturbed by the material whirlpool, by his affection for his family, society, and community. Thus Arjuna wanted to become a philanthropic, nonviolent man of the world. However, when he became *budha* by hearing the Vedic knowledge of *Bhagavad-gītā* from the Supreme Person, he changed his decision and became a worshiper of Lord Śrī Kṛṣṇa, who had Himself designed the Battle of Kurukṣetra. Arjuna worshiped the Lord by fighting with his so-called relatives. In this way he became a pure devotee of the Lord. Such accomplishments are possible only when one worships the real Kṛṣṇa and not some fabricated "Kṛṣṇa" invented by foolish men who are without knowledge of the intricacies of the science of Kṛṣṇa described in *Bhagavad-gītā* and *Śrīmad-Bhāgavatam.*

According to *Vedānta-sūtra, sambhūta* is the source of birth and sustenance as well as the reservoir that remains after annihilation. The *Śrīmad-Bhāgavatam*, the natural commentary upon *Vedānta-sūtra* by the same author, maintains that the source of all emanations is not like a dead stone but is *abhijña*, or fully conscious. The primeval Lord Śrī Kṛṣṇa also says in *Bhagavad-gītā* (7.26) that He is fully conscious of past, present, and future and that no one, including demigods such as Śiva and Brahmā, knows Him fully. Certainly those who are disturbed by the tides of material existence cannot know Him fully. Half-educated spiritual masters try to make some compromise by making the mass of humanity the object of worship, but they do not know that such worship is not possible and that the masses are not perfect. Their attempt is something like pouring water on the leaves of a tree instead of the root. The natural process is to pour water on the root, but today's disturbed leaders are more attached to the leaves. Despite their perpetually watering the leaves, everything is drying up for want of nourishment.

Śrī Īśopaniṣad advises us to pour water on the root, the source of all germination. Worship of the mass of humanity by rendering bodily service, which can never be perfect, is less important than service to the soul. The soul is the root that generates different types of bodies according to the law of *karma*, material reaction. To serve human beings by medical aid, social help, and educational facilities while at the same time cutting the throats of poor animals in slaughterhouses is not really valid service to living beings.

The living being is perpetually suffering in different types of bodies from the material miseries of birth, old age, disease, and death. The human form of life offers one a chance to get out of this entanglement simply by reestablishing the lost relationship between the living entity and the Supreme Lord. The Lord comes personally to teach this philosophy of surrender unto the Supreme, the *sambhūta.* Real service to humanity is rendered when one teaches surrender to and worship of the Supreme Lord with full love and energy. That is the instruction of *Śrī Īśopaniṣad* in this *mantra.*

The simple way to worship the Supreme Lord in this age of disturbance is to hear and chant about His great activities. The mental speculators, however, think that the activities of the Lord are imaginary; therefore they refrain from hearing of them and invent some word jugglery without substance to divert the attention of the innocent masses of people. Instead of hearing of the activities of Lord Kṛṣṇa, they advertise themselves by inducing their followers to sing about pseudo spiritual masters. In modern times the number of such pretenders has increased considerably, and it has become a problem for the pure devotees of the Lord to save the masses of people from the unholy propaganda of these pretenders and pseudoincarnations.

The *Upaniṣads* indirectly draw our attention to the primeval Lord Śrī Kṛṣṇa, but *Bhagavad-gītā,* which is the summary of all the *Upaniṣads*, directly points to Śrī Kṛṣṇa. By hearing about Kṛṣṇa as He is in *Bhagavad-gītā* or *Śrīmad-Bhāgavatam*, one's mind is gradually cleansed of all contaminated things. *Śrīmad-Bhāgavatam* says, "By hearing of the activities of the Lord, one draws the attention of the Lord toward His devotee. Thus the Lord, being situated in the heart of every living being, helps the devotee by giving him proper directions." *Bhagavad-gītā* (10.10) also confirms this.

The Lord's inner direction cleanses the heart of the devotee of all contamination produced by the material modes of passion and ignorance. Nondevotees are under the sway of passion and ignorance. One who is in passion cannot become detached from material hankering, and one in ignorance cannot know what he is nor what the Lord is. Thus when one is in passion or ignorance, there is no chance for self-realization, however much one may play the part of a religionist. For a devotee, the modes of passion and ignorance are removed by the grace of the Lord. In this way the devotee becomes situated in the quality of goodness, the sign of a perfect *brāhmaṇa*. Everyone and anyone can qualify as a *brāhmaṇa* provided he follows the path of devotional service under the guidance of a bona fide spiritual master. *Śrīmad-Bhāgavatam* (2.4.18) also says,

kirāta-hūṇāndhra-pulinda-pulkaśā
ābhīra-śumbhā yavanāḥ khasādayaḥ
ye 'nye ca pāpā yad-apāśrayāśrayāḥ
śudhyanti tasmai prabhaviṣṇave namaḥ

Any lowborn living entity can be purified by the guidance of a pure devotee of the Lord, for the Lord is extraordinarily powerful.

When one attains brahminical qualifications, he becomes happy and enthusiastic to render devotional service to the

Lord. Automatically the science of God is unveiled before him. By knowing the science of God, one gradually becomes freed from material attachments, and one's doubtful mind becomes crystal clear by the grace of the Lord. When one attains this stage, he can become a liberated soul and see the Lord in every step of life. This is the perfection of *sambhavāt*, as described in this *mantra*.

MANTRA FOURTEEN

सम्भूतिं च विनाशं च यस्तद् वेदोभयं॰ सह ।
विनाशेन मृत्युं तीर्त्वा सम्भूत्यामृतमश्नुते ॥ १४ ॥

sambhūtiṁ ca vināśaṁ ca
yas tad vedobhayaṁ saha
vināśena mṛtyuṁ tīrtvā
sambhūtyāmṛtam aśnute

sambhūtim—the eternal Personality of Godhead; His transcendental name, form, pastimes, qualities, and paraphernalia; the variegatedness of His abode, etc.; *ca*—and; *vināśam*—the temporary material manifestation of demigods, men, animals, etc., with their false names, fame, etc.; *ca*—also; *yaḥ*—one who; *tat*—that; *veda*—knows; *ubhayam*—both; *saha*—along with; *vināśena*—with everything liable to be vanquished; *mṛtyum*—death; *tīrtvā*—surpassing; *sambhūtyā*—in the eternal kingdom of God; *amṛtam*—deathlessness; *aśnute*—enjoys.

TRANSLATION

One should know perfectly the Personality of Godhead and His transcendental name, as well as the temporary material creation with its temporary demigods, men, and animals. When one knows these, he surpasses death and the ephemeral cosmic manifestation with it, and in the eternal kingdom of God he enjoys his eternal life of bliss and knowledge.

PURPORT

By its so-called advancement of knowledge, human civilization has created many material things, including spaceships and atomic energy. Yet it has failed to create freedom from birth, old age, disease, and death. Whenever an intelligent man raises the question of these miseries before a so-called scientist, the scientist very cleverly replies that material science is progressing and that it will ultimately be possible to render man deathless and ageless. Such answers prove the scientists' gross ignorance of material nature. In material nature, everything is under the stringent laws of matter and must pass through six stages of transformation: birth, growth, maintenance, transformation, deterioration, and finally death. Nothing that is in contact with material nature can be beyond these six laws of transformation; therefore no one—whether demigod, man, animal, or tree—can survive forever in the material world.

The duration of life may vary according to species. Lord Brahmā, the chief living being within this material universe, may live for millions and millions of years, while a minute germ may live for some hours only. But that does not matter. No one in the material world can survive eternally. Things are born or created under certain conditions, they stay for some time, and if they continue to live, they grow, procreate, gradually dwindle, and finally vanish. According to these laws, even the Brahmās, of which there are millions in different universes, are all liable to death either today or tomorrow. Therefore the entire material universe is called Mṛtyuloka, the place of death.

Material scientists and politicians are trying to make this place deathless, because they have no information of the deathless spiritual nature. This is due to their ignorance of Vedic literature, which is full of knowledge of mature transcendental experience. Unfortunately, modern man is averse to receiving knowledge from the *Vedas*, *Purāṇas*, and other scriptures.

From *Viṣṇu Purāṇa* (6.7.61) we receive information that Lord Viṣṇu, the Personality of Godhead, possesses different energies, known as *parā* (superior) and *aparā* or *avidyā* (inferior). The material energy, in which we are presently entangled, is called the *avidyā*, or inferior, energy. The material creation is made possible by this energy. Yet there is another, a superior, energy called the *parā śakti*, which is different from this material, inferior energy. That superior energy constitutes the eternal, or deathless, creation of the Lord (Bg. 8.20).

All the material planets—upper, lower, and intermediate, including the sun, moon, and Venus—are scattered throughout the universe. These planets exist only during the lifetime of Brahmā. Some lower planets, however, are vanquished after the end of one day of Brahmā and are again created during the next day of Brahmā. On the upper planets, time is calculated differently. One of our years is equal to only twenty-four hours, or one day and night, on many of the upper planets. The four ages of earth (Satya, Tretā, Dvāpara, and Kali) last only twelve thousand years according to the time scale of the upper planets. Such a length of time multiplied by one thousand constitutes one day of Brahmā, and one night of Brahmā is the same. Such days and nights accumulate into months and years, and Brahmā lives for one hundred such years. At the end of Brahmā's life, the complete universal manifestation is vanquished.

Those living beings who reside in the sun and on the moon, as well as those in the Martyaloka system—which includes this earth and many planets below it—are all merged into the waters of devastation during the night of Brahmā.

During this time no living beings or species remain manifest, although spiritually they continue to exist. This unmanifested state is called *avyakta.* Again, when the entire universe is vanquished at the end of Brahmā's lifetime, there is another *avyakta* state. However, beyond these two unmanifested states is a spiritual atmosphere or nature. There are a great number of spiritual planets in this atmosphere, and these planets exist eternally, even when all the planets within this material universe are vanquished. The cosmic manifestation within the jurisdiction of the various Brahmās is but a display of one fourth of the energy of the Lord. This is the inferior energy. Beyond the jurisdiction of Brahmā is the spiritual nature, which is called *tri-pād-vibhūti,* three fourths of the Lord's energy. This is the superior energy, or *parā prakṛti.*

The predominating Supreme Person residing within the spiritual nature is Lord Śrī Kṛṣṇa. As confirmed in *Bhagavad-gītā* (8.22), He can be approached only by unalloyed devotional service and not by the processes of *jñāna* (philosophy), *yoga* (mysticism), or *karma* (fruitive work). The *karmīs,* or fruitive workers, can elevate themselves to the Svargaloka planets, which include the sun and moon. *Jñānīs* and *yogīs* can attain still higher planets, such as Brahmaloka, and when they become still more qualified through devotional service, they are allowed to enter into the spiritual nature—either the illuminating cosmic atmosphere of the spiritual sky (Brahman) or the Vaikuṇṭha planets, according to their qualification. It is certain, however, that no one can enter into the spiritual, Vaikuṇṭha planets without being trained in devotional service.

On the material planets, everyone from Brahmā down to the ant is trying to lord it over material nature, and this is the material disease. As long as this material disease continues, the living entity has to undergo the process of bodily change. Whether he takes the form of a man, demigod, or animal, he ultimately has to endure an unmanifested condition during the two devastations—the devastation of the night of Brahmā and the devastation at the end of Brahmā's life. If we want to put an end to this process of repeated birth and death, as well as to the concomitant factors of old age and disease, we must try to enter the spiritual planets. Lord Kṛṣṇa in His plenary expansions dominates each and every one of these planets.

No one can dominate Kṛṣṇa. It is the conditioned soul who tries to dominate material nature and is instead subjected to the laws of material nature and the sufferings of repeated birth and death. The Lord comes here to reestablish the principles of religion, and the basic principle is the development of an attitude of surrender to Him. This is the Lord's last instruction in *Bhagavad-gītā* (18.66), but foolish men have tactfully misinterpreted this prime teaching and have misled the masses of people in diverse ways. People have been urged to open hospitals but not to educate themselves to enter into the spiritual kingdom by devotional service. They have been taught to take interest only in temporary relief work, which can never bring real happiness to the living entity. They start varieties of public and semigovernmental institutions to tackle the devastating power of nature, but they don't know how to pacify insurmountable nature. Many men are advertised as great scholars of *Bhagavad-gītā*, but they overlook the *Gītā's* message, by which material nature can be pacified. Powerful nature can only be pacified by the awakening of God consciousness, as clearly pointed out in *Bhagavad-gītā* (7.14).

In this *mantra*, *Śrī Īśopaniṣad* teaches that one must know both *sambhūti* (the Personality of Godhead) and *vināśa* (the temporary material manifestation) perfectly, side by side. By knowing the temporary material manifestation alone, one cannot save anything, for in the course of nature there is devastation at every moment. No one can be saved from these devastations by opening hospitals. One can be saved only by complete knowledge of the eternal life of bliss and awareness. The whole Vedic scheme is meant to educate men in this art of attaining eternal life. People are often misguided by temporary attractive things based on sense gratification, but service rendered to the objects of the senses is both misleading and degrading.

We must therefore save our fellow man in the right way. There is no question of liking or disliking the truth. It is there. If we want to be saved from repeated birth and death, we must take to the devotional service of the Lord. There can be no compromise, for this is a matter of necessity.

MANTRA FIFTEEN

हिरण्मयेन पात्रेण सत्यस्यापिहितं मुखम् ।
तत् त्वं पूषन्नपावृणु सत्यधर्माय दृष्टये ॥ १५ ॥

hiraṇmayena pātreṇa
satyasyāpihitaṁ mukham
tat tvaṁ pūṣann apāvṛṇu
satya-dharmāyā dṛṣṭaye

hiraṇmayena—by a golden effulgence; *pātreṇa*—by dazzling covering; *satyasya*—of the Supreme Truth; *apihitam*—covered; *mukham*—the face; *tat*—that covering; *tvam*—Yourself; *pūṣan*—O sustainer; *apāvṛṇu*—kindly remove; *satya*—pure; *dharmāya*—unto the devotee; *dṛṣṭaye*—for exhibiting.

TRANSLATION

O my Lord, sustainer of all that lives, Your real face is covered by Your dazzling effulgence. Please remove that covering and exhibit Yourself to Your pure devotee.

PURPORT

In *Bhagavad-gītā* (14.27), the Lord explains His personal rays (*brahmajyoti*), the dazzling effulgence of His personal form, in this way:

brahmaṇo hi pratiṣṭhāham
amṛtasyāvyayasya ca
śāśvatasya ca dharmasya
sukhasyaikāntikasya ca

"And I am the basis of the impersonal Brahman, which is the constitutional position of ultimate happiness, and which is immortal, imperishable, and eternal."

Brahman, Paramātmā, and Bhagavān are three aspects of the same Absolute Truth. Brahman is the aspect most easily perceived by the beginner. Paramātmā, the Supersoul, is realized by those who have further progressed, and Bhagavān realization is the ultimate realization of the Absolute Truth. This is confirmed in *Bhagavad-gītā*, where the Lord says that He is the ultimate concept of the Absolute Truth, the source of the *brahmajyoti* as well as the all-pervading Paramātmā. In *Bhagavad-gītā* Kṛṣṇa says that He is the ultimate reservoir of the *brahmajyoti*, the impersonal conception of the Absolute Truth, and that there is no need to explain His unlimited potencies.

atha vā bahunaitena
kiṁ jñātena tavārjuna
viṣṭabhyāham idaṁ kṛtsnam
ekāṁśena sthito jagat

"But what need is there, Arjuna, for all this detailed knowledge? With a single fragment of Myself I pervade and support this entire universe." (Bg. 10.42) Thus by His one plenary expansion, the all-pervading Paramātmā, the Lord maintains the complete material cosmic creation. He also maintains all manifestations in the spiritual world as well;

therefore, in the *śruti-mantra* of *Śrī Īśopaniṣad*, the Lord is addressed as *pūṣan*, the ultimate maintainer.

The Personality of Godhead, Śrī Kṛṣṇa, is always in transcendental bliss (*ānanda-mayo 'bhyāsāt*). When He was present at Vṛndāvana in India five thousand years ago, He always remained in transcendental bliss, even from the beginning of His childhood pastimes. The killings of varieties of demons—such as Agha, Baka, Pūtanā, and Pralamba—were but pleasure excursions for Him. In the village of Vṛndāvana He enjoyed Himself with His mother, brother, and friends, and when He played the role of a naughty butter thief, all His associates enjoyed celestial bliss by His stealing. The Lord's fame as a butter thief is not reproachable, for by stealing butter the Lord gave pleasure to His pure devotees. Everything that was performed by the Lord at Vṛndāvana was performed for the pleasure of His associates there. The Lord created these pastimes to attract the dry speculators and the acrobats of the so-called *haṭha-yoga* system who had come to find the Absolute Truth.

Of the childhood play between the Lord and His playmates, the cowherd boys, Śukadeva Gosvāmī said in *Śrīmad-Bhāgavatam* (10.12.11),

itthaṁ satāṁ brahma-sukhānubhūtyā
dāsyaṁ gatānāṁ para-daivatena
māyāśritānāṁ nara-dārakeṇa
sākaṁ vijahruḥ kṛta-puṇya-puñjāḥ

"The Personality of Godhead, who is perceived as the impersonal, blissful Brahman, who is worshiped as the Supreme Lord by the devotees, and who is considered an ordinary human being by the mundane, played with the cowherd boys, who had attained their position after accumulating many pious activities."

Thus the Lord is always engaged in transcendental loving activities with His spiritual associates in the various relationships of *śānta* (neutrality), *dāsya* (servitorship), *sakhya* (friendship), *vātsalya* (paternal affection), and *mādhurya* (conjugal love).

Since it is said that the Lord never leaves Vṛndāvana-dhāma, one may ask how He manages the affairs of the creation. This is answered in *Bhagavad-gītā* (13.14): the Lord pervades the entire material creation by His plenary part known as the *puruṣa* incarnation. Although the Lord personally has nothing to do with material creation, maintenance, and destruction, He causes all these things to be done by His plenary expansion, the Paramātmā, or Supersoul. Every living entity is known as *ātmā*, soul, and the principal *ātmā* who controls them all is Paramātmā, the Supersoul.

This system of God realization is a great science. The materialists can only analyze and meditate on the twenty-four factors of the material creation, for they have very little information of the *puruṣa*, the Lord. The impersonal transcendentalists are simply bewildered by the glaring effulgence of the *brahmajyoti*. If one wants to see the Absolute Truth in full, he has to penetrate beyond the twenty-four material elements and the glaring effulgence as well. *Śrī Īśopaniṣad* points toward this direction, praying for the removal of the *hiraṇmaya-pātra*, the dazzling covering. Unless this covering is removed so one can perceive the Personality of Godhead as He is, factual realization of the Absolute Truth can never be attained.

The Paramātmā feature of the Personality of Godhead is one of three plenary expansions, collectively called *viṣṇu-tattva*. The *viṣṇu-tattva* within the universe (one of the three principal deities: Brahmā, Viṣṇu, and Śiva) is known as the Kṣīrodakaśāyī Viṣṇu. He is the all-pervading Paramātmā in each and every individual living entity. The Garbhodakaśāyī Viṣṇu is the collective Supersoul within all living entities. Beyond these two is the Kāraṇodakaśāyī Viṣṇu lying in the Causal Ocean. He is the creator of all universes. The *yoga* system teaches the serious student to meet the *viṣṇu-tattvas* after overcoming the twenty-four material elements of the cosmic creation. The culture of empiric philosophy helps one realize the impersonal *brahmajyoti*, which is the glaring effulgence of the transcendental body of Lord Śrī Kṛṣṇa. This is confirmed in *Bhagavad-gītā* (14.27), as well as *Brahma-saṁhitā* (5.40):

yasya prabhā prabhavato jagad-aṇḍa-koṭi-
koṭiṣv aśeṣa-vasudhādi vibhūti-bhinnam
tad brahma niṣkalam anantam aśeṣa-bhūtaṁ
govindam ādi-puruṣaṁ tam ahaṁ bhajāmi

"In the millions and millions of universes, there are innumerable planets, and each and every one of them is different from the others by its cosmic constitution. All of these planets are situated in a corner of the *brahmajyoti*. This *brahmajyoti* is but the personal rays of the Supreme Personality of Godhead, whom I worship." This *mantra* from *Brahma-saṁhitā* is spoken from the platform of factual realization of the Absolute Truth, and the *śruti-mantra* of *Śrī Īśopaniṣad* confirms this *mantra* as a process of realization. It is a simple prayer to the Lord to remove the *brahmajyoti* so that one can see His real face.

Perfect knowledge means knowing Kṛṣṇa as the root of Brahman. The root of Brahman is Lord Śrī Kṛṣṇa, and in scriptures such as *Śrīmad-Bhāgavatam* the science of Kṛṣṇa is perfectly elaborated. In *Śrīmad-Bhāgavatam* the author, Śrīla Vyāsadeva, has established that the Supreme Truth is described as Brahman, Paramātmā, or Bhagavān according to one's realization of Him. Śrīla Vyāsadeva never states that the Supreme Truth is a *jīva*, an ordinary living entity. The living entity should never be considered the all-powerful Supreme Truth. If he were, there would be no need for the living entity to pray to the Lord to remove His dazzling cover so that the living entity can see His real form.

The conclusion is that in the absence of spiritually potent manifestations of the Supreme Truth, the impersonal Brahman is realized. Similarly, when one realizes the material potencies of the Lord, having little or no information of the spiritual potency, he attains Paramātmā realization. Thus both Brahman and Paramātmā realization of the Absolute Truth are partial realizations. However, when one realizes the Supreme Personality of Godhead, Śrī Kṛṣṇa, in full potency after the removal of the *hiraṇmaya-pātra*, he realizes *vāsudevaḥ sarvam iti:* Lord Śrī Kṛṣṇa, known as Vāsudeva, is everything—Brahman, Paramātmā, and Bhagavān. He is Bhagavān, the root, and Brahman and Paramātmā are His branches.

In *Bhagavad-gītā* there is a comparative analysis of the three types of transcendentalists—the worshipers of the impersonal Brahman (*jñānīs*), the worshipers of the Paramātmā feature (*yogīs*), and the devotees of Lord Śrī Kṛṣṇa (*bhaktas*). It is stated in *Bhagavad-gītā* (6.46–47) that among all types of transcendentalists, he who is a *jñānī*, who has cultivated Vedic knowledge, is supreme. Yet the *yogīs* are still greater than the *jñānīs* and far superior to fruitive workers as well. And among all *yogīs*, he who constantly serves the Lord with all his energies is the topmost. In summary, a philosopher is better than a laboring man, and a mystic is superior to a philosopher. And of all the mystic *yogīs*, he who follows *bhakti-yoga*, constantly engaged in the service of the Lord, is the highest. *Śrī Īśopaniṣad* directs us toward this perfection.

MANTRA SIXTEEN

पूषन्नेकर्षे यम सूर्य प्राजापत्य व्यूह रश्मीन् समूह
तेजो यत् ते रूपं कल्याणतमं तत् ते पश्यामि
योऽसावसौ पुरुषः सोऽहमस्मि ॥ १६ ॥

pūṣann ekarṣe yama sūrya prājāpatya vyūha raśmīn samūha
tejo yat te rūpaṁ kalyāṇatamaṁ tat te paśyāmi
yo 'sāv asau puruṣaḥ so 'ham asmi

pūṣan—O maintainer; *ekarṣe*—the primeval philosopher; *yama*—the regulating principle; *sūrya*—the destination of the *sūris* (great devotees); *prājāpatya*—the well-wisher of the Prajāpatis (progenitors of mankind); *vyūha*—kindly remove; *raśmīn*—the rays; *samūha*—kindly withdraw; *tejaḥ*—effulgence; *yat*—so that; *te*—Your; *rūpam*—form; *kalyāṇa-tamam*—most auspicious; *tat*—that; *te*—Your; *paśyāmi*—I may see; *yaḥ*—one who is; *asau*—like the sun; *asau*—that; *puruṣaḥ*—Personality of Godhead; *saḥ*—myself; *aham*—I; *asmi*—am.

TRANSLATION

O my Lord, O primeval philosopher, maintainer of the universe, O regulating principle, destination of the pure devotees, well-wisher of the progenitors of mankind—please remove the effulgence of Your transcendental rays so that I can see Your form of bliss. You are the eternal Supreme Personality of Godhead, like unto the sun, as am I.

PURPORT

The sun and its rays are one and the same qualitatively. Similarly, the Lord and the living entities are one and the same in quality. The sun is one, but the molecules of the sun's rays are innumerable. The sun's rays constitute part of the sun, and the sun and its rays conjointly constitute the complete sun. Within the sun itself resides the sun-god, and similarly within the supreme spiritual planet, Goloka Vṛndāvana, from which the *brahmajyoti* effulgence is emanating, resides the eternal Lord, as verified by *Brahma-saṁhitā* (5.29):

cintāmaṇi-prakara-sadmasu kalpa-vṛkṣa-
lakṣāvṛteṣu surabhīr abhipālayantam
lakṣmī-sahasra-śata-sambhrama-sevyamānaṁ
govindam ādi-puruṣaṁ tam ahaṁ bhajāmi

"I worship Govinda, the primeval Lord, the first progenitor, who is tending the cows, fulfilling all desires in abodes filled with spiritual gems, surrounded by millions of wish-fulfilling trees, always served with great reverence and affection by hundreds of thousands of Lakṣmīs, or goddesses of fortune."

The *brahmajyoti* is also described in *Brahma-saṁhitā*, where it is said that the *brahmajyoti* is the rays emanating from that supreme spiritual planet, Goloka Vṛndāvana, just as the sun's rays emanate from the sun globe. Until one surpasses the glare of the *brahmajyoti*, he cannot receive information of the land of the Lord. Being blinded by the dazzling *brahmajyoti*, the impersonalist philosopher can neither realize the factual abode of the Lord nor His transcendental form. Limited by their poor fund of knowledge, such impersonalist thinkers cannot understand the all-blissful, transcendental form of Lord Kṛṣṇa. In this prayer, therefore, *Śrī Īśopaniṣad* petitions the Lord to remove the effulgent rays of the *brahmajyoti* so that the pure devotee can see His all-blissful, transcendental form.

By realizing the impersonal *brahmajyoti*, one experiences the auspicious aspect of the Supreme, and by realizing the Paramātmā, or all-pervading feature of the Supreme, one experiences an even more auspicious enlightenment. By meeting the Personality of Godhead Himself face to face, the devotee experiences the most auspicious feature of the Supreme. Since He is addressed as the primeval philosopher and maintainer and well-wisher of the universe, the Supreme Truth cannot be considered impersonal. This is the verdict of *Śrī Īśopaniṣad*. The word *pūṣan* ("maintainer") is especially significant, for although the Lord maintains all beings, He specifically maintains His devotees. After surpassing the impersonal *brahmajyoti* and seeing the personal aspect of the Lord and His most auspicious, eternal form, the devotee realizes the Absolute Truth in full.

In *Bhagavat-sandarbha*, Śrīla Jīva Gosvāmī states, "The complete conception of the Absolute Truth is realized in the Personality of Godhead because He is almighty and possesses full transcendental potencies. The full potency of the Absolute Truth is not realized in the *brahmajyoti*; therefore Brahman realization is only partial realization of the Personality of Godhead. O learned sages, the first letter of the word *bhagavān* is twice significant: first in the sense of 'one who fully maintains' and second in the sense of 'guardian.' The second letter (*ga*) means 'guide,' 'leader,' or 'creator.' The letter *va* indicates that every being lives in Him and that He also lives in every being. In other words, the transcendental sound *bhagavān* represents infinite knowledge, potency, energy, opulence, strength, and influence—all without a tinge of material inebriety."

The Lord fully maintains His unalloyed devotees, and He guides them progressively on the path of devotional perfection. As the leader of His devotees, He ultimately awards the desired results of devotional service by giving Himself to them. The devotees of the Lord see the Lord face to face by the causeless mercy of the Lord; thus the Lord helps His devotees reach the supermost spiritual planet, Goloka Vṛndāvana. Being the creator, He can bestow all necessary qualifications upon His devotee so that the devotee can ultimately reach Him. The Lord is the cause of all causes, and since there is nothing that caused Him, He is the original cause. Consequently He enjoys His own Self by manifesting His own internal potency. The external potency is not exactly manifested by Himself, for He expands Himself as the *puruṣas*, and it is in these forms that He maintains the features of the material manifestation. By such expansions, He creates, maintains, and annihilates the cosmic manifestation.

The living entities are also differentiated expansions of the Lord's Self, and because some of them desire to be lords and imitate the Supreme Lord, He allows them to enter into the cosmic creation with the option to fully utilize their propensity to lord it over nature. Due to the presence of His parts and parcels, the living entities, the entire phenomenal world is stirred into action and reaction. Thus the living entities are given full facility to lord it over material nature, but the ultimate controller is the Lord Himself in His plenary feature as Paramātmā, the Supersoul, which is one of the *puruṣas*.

Thus there is a gulf of difference between the living entity (*ātmā*) and the controlling Lord (Paramātmā), the soul and the Supersoul. Paramātmā is the controller, and *ātmā* is the controlled; therefore they cannot exist on the same level. Because the Paramātmā fully cooperates with the *ātmā*, He is known as the constant companion of the living being.

The all-pervading feature of the Lord—which exists in all circumstances of waking and sleeping as well as in potential states and from which the *jīva-śakti* (living force) is generated as both conditioned and liberated souls—is known as Brahman. Since the Lord is the origin of both Paramātmā and Brahman, He is the origin of all living entities and all else that exists. One who knows this engages himself at once in the devotional service of the Lord. Such a pure and fully cognizant devotee of the Lord is fully attached to Him in heart and soul, and whenever such a devotee assembles with similar devotees, they have no engagement but the glorification of the Lord's transcendental activities. Those who are not as perfect as the pure devotees and those who have realized only the Brahman or Paramātmā features of the Lord cannot appreciate the activities of the perfect devotees. The Lord always helps the pure devotees by imparting necessary knowledge within their hearts; thus by His special favor all the darkness of ignorance is dissipated. The speculative philosophers and *yogīs* cannot imagine this, because they more or less depend on their own strength. As stated in *Kaṭha Upaniṣad,* the Lord can be known only by those whom He favors, and not by anyone else. Such special favors are bestowed upon His pure devotees only. *Śrī Īśopaniṣad* thus points to the favor of the Lord, which is beyond the purview of the *brahmajyoti.*

MANTRA SEVENTEEN

वायुरनिलममृतमथेदं भस्मान्तं शरीरम् ।
ॐ क्रतो स्मर कृतं स्मर क्रतो स्मर कृतं स्मर ॥ १७ ॥

vāyur anilam amṛtam
athedaṁ bhasmāntaṁ śarīram
oṁ krato smara kṛtaṁ smara
krato smara kṛtaṁ smara

vāyuḥ—air of life; *anilam*—total reservoir of air; *amṛtam*—indestructible; *atha*—now; *idam*—this; *bhasmāntam*—after being turned to ashes; *śarīram*—body; *oṁ*—O Lord; *krataḥ*—the enjoyer of all sacrifices; *smara*—please remember; *kṛtam*—all that has been done by me; *smara*—please remember; *krataḥ*—the supreme beneficiary; *smara*—please remember; *kṛtam*—all that I have done for You; *smara*—please remember.

TRANSLATION

Let this temporary body be burned to ashes, and let the air of life be merged with the totality of air. Now, O my Lord, please remember all my sacrifices, and because You are the ultimate beneficiary, please remember all that I have done for You.

PURPORT

This temporary material body is certainly a foreign dress. In *Bhagavad-gītā* (2.13, 18.30) it is clearly said that after the destruction of the material body the living entity is not annihilated, nor does he lose his identity. The identity of the living entity is never impersonal or formless; on the contrary, it is the material dress that is formless and which takes a shape according to the form of the indestructible person. No living entity is originally formless, as is wrongly thought by those with a poor fund of knowledge. This *mantra* verifies the fact that the living entity exists after the annihilation of the material body.

In the material world, material nature displays wonderful workmanship by creating different varieties of bodies for the living beings in accordance with their propensities for sense gratification. The living entity who wants to taste stool is given a material body that is quite suitable for eating stool—that of a hog. Similarly, one who wants to eat meat is given the body of a tiger, by which he can live by enjoying the blood of other animals and eating their flesh. Because the shape of his teeth is different, the human being is not meant for eating stool or flesh, nor does he have any desire to taste stool, even in his most aboriginal state. Human teeth are so made that they can chew and cut fruit and vegetables, and two canine teeth are also given so that one can eat flesh.

The material bodies of all animals and men are foreign to the living entity. They change according to the living entity's desire for sense gratification. In the cycle of evolution, the living entity changes bodies one after another. When the world was full of water, the living entity took an aquatic form. Then he passed from vegetable life to worm life, from worm life to bird life, from bird life to animal life, and from animal life into the human form. The highest developed form is this human form when it is possessed of a full sense of spiritual knowledge. The highest development of one's spiritual sense is described in this *mantra:* one should give up this material body, which will be turned to ashes, and allow the air of life to merge into the eternal reservoir of air. The living being's activities are performed within the body through the movements of different kinds of air, known in summary as *prāṇa-vāyu.* The *yogīs* generally study to control the airs of the body. The soul is supposed to rise from one circle of air to another until it rises to the *brahma-randhra,* the highest circle. From that point the perfect *yogī* can transfer himself to any desired planet. The process is to give up one material body and then enter into another, but the highest perfection of such changes is possible only when the living entity is able to give up the material body altogether, as suggested in this *mantra.* He may then enter into the spiritual atmosphere, where he can develop a completely different type of body—a spiritual body, which never has to meet death or change.

In the material world material nature forces one to change his body due to his different desires for sense gratification. These desires are represented in the various species of life from germs to the most perfected material bodies—those of Brahmā and the demigods. All of these living entities have bodies composed of matter in different shapes. The intelligent man sees oneness not in the variety of the bodies but in the spiritual identity. The spiritual spark which is the part and parcel of the Supreme Lord is the same whether he is in a body of a hog or in the body of a demigod. The living entity takes on different bodies according to his pious and vicious activities. The human body is highly developed and has full consciousness. According to the Vedic scriptures, the most perfect man surrenders unto the Lord after many, many lifetimes of culturing knowledge. The culture of knowledge reaches perfection only when the knower comes to the point of surrendering unto the Supreme Lord, Vāsudeva. Yet even after attaining knowledge of one's spiritual identity, if one does not come to the point of knowing that the living entities are eternal parts and parcels of the whole and can never become the whole, one has to fall down again into the material atmosphere. Indeed, one must fall down even if he has become one with the *brahmajyoti.*

The *brahmajyoti* emanating from the transcendental body of the Lord is full of spiritual sparks that are individual entities with the full sense of existence. Sometimes these living entities want to become enjoyers of the senses, and therefore they are placed in the material world to become false lords under the dictation of the senses. The desire for lordship is the material disease of the living being, for under the spell of sense enjoyment he transmigrates through the various bodies manifested in the material world. Becoming one with the *brahmajyoti* does not represent mature knowledge. Only by surrendering unto the Lord completely and developing one's sense of spiritual service does one reach the highest perfectional stage.

In this *mantra* the living entity prays to enter the spiritual kingdom of God after relinquishing his material body and material air. The devotee prays to the Lord to remember his activities and the sacrifices he has performed before his material body is turned into ashes. This prayer is made at the time of death with full consciousness of one's past deeds and of the ultimate goal. One who is completely under the rule of material nature remembers the heinous activities performed during the existence of his material body and consequently gets another material body after death. *Bhagavad-gītā* (8.6) confirms this truth:

yaṁ yaṁ vāpi smaran bhāvaṁ
tyajaty ante kalevaram

taṁ tam evaiti kaunteya
sadā tad-bhāva-bhāvitaḥ

"Whatever state of being one remembers when he quits his body, that state he will attain without fail." Thus the mind carries the propensities of the dying animal into the next life.

Unlike the simple animals, who have no developed mind, the human being can remember the activities of his passing life like dreams at night; therefore his mind remains surcharged with material desires, and consequently he cannot enter into the spiritual kingdom with a spiritual body. However, the devotees develop a sense of love for Godhead by practicing devotional service to the Lord. Even if a devotee does not remember his godly service at the time of death, the Lord does not forget him. This prayer is given to remind the Lord of the devotee's sacrifices, but even if there is no such reminder, the Lord does not forget the devotional service of His pure devotee.

The Lord clearly describes His intimate relationship with His devotees in *Bhagavad-gītā* (9.30–34): "Even if one commits the most abominable actions, if he is engaged in devotional service he is to be considered saintly because he is properly situated. He quickly becomes righteous and attains lasting peace. O son of Kuntī, declare it boldly that My devotee never perishes. O son of Pṛthā, those who take shelter in Me, though they be of lower birth—women, *vaiśyas* [merchants] as well as *śūdras* [workers]—can approach the supreme destination. How much greater then are the *brāhmaṇas*, the righteous, the devotees, and the saintly kings, who in this temporary, miserable world engage in loving service unto Me. Engage your mind always in thinking of Me, offer obeisances and worship Me. Being completely absorbed in Me, surely you will come to Me."

Śrīla Bhaktivinoda Ṭhākura explains these verses in this

way: "One should accept a devotee who is on the right path of the saints, even though such a devotee may seem to be of loose character. One should try to understand the real purport of the words 'loose character.' A conditioned soul has to act for double functions—namely for the maintenance of the body and again for self-realization. Social status, mental development, cleanliness, austerity, nourishment, and the struggle for existence are all for the maintenance of the body. The self-realization part of one's activities is executed in one's occupation as a devotee of the Lord, and one performs action in that connection also. These two different functions parallel one another, because a conditioned soul cannot give up the maintenance of his body. The proportion of activities for maintenance of the body decreases, however, in proportion to the increase in devotional service. As long as the proportion of devotional service does not come to the right point, there is a chance for an occasional exhibition of worldliness, but it should be noted that such worldliness cannot continue for any length of time because, by the grace of the Lord, such imperfections will come to an end very shortly. Therefore the path of devotional service is the only right path. If one is on the right path, even an occasional occurrence of worldliness does not hamper one in the advancement of self-realization."

The facilities of devotional service are denied the impersonalists because they are attached to the *brahmajyoti* feature of the Lord. As suggested in the previous *mantras*, they cannot penetrate the *brahmajyoti*, because they do not believe in the Personality of Godhead. Their business is mostly semantics, the jugglery of words, and mental creations. Consequently the impersonalists pursue a fruitless labor, as confirmed in the Twelfth Chapter of *Bhagavad-gītā* (12.5).

All the facilities suggested in this *mantra* can be easily obtained by constant contact with the personal feature of the

Absolute Truth. Devotional service to the Lord consists essentially of nine transcendental activities performed by the devotee: (1) hearing about the Lord, (2) glorifying the Lord, (3) remembering the Lord, (4) serving the lotus feet of the Lord, (5) worshiping the Lord, (6) offering prayers to the Lord, (7) serving the Lord, (8) enjoying friendly association with the Lord, and (9) surrendering everything unto the Lord. These nine principles of devotional service—taken altogether or one by one—can help a devotee to remain constantly in touch with God. In this way, at the end of life it is easy for the devotee to remember the Lord. By adopting only one of these nine principles it was possible for the following renowned devotees of the Lord to achieve the highest perfection. (1) By hearing, Mahārāja Parīkṣit, the hero of *Śrīmad-Bhāgavatam*, attained the desired result. (2) Just by glorifying the Lord, Śukadeva Gosvāmī, the speaker of *Śrīmad-Bhāgavatam*, attained his perfection. (3) By praying, Akrūra attained the desired result. (4) By remembering, Prahlāda Mahārāja attained the desired result. (5) By worshiping, Pṛthu Mahārāja attained perfection. (6) By serving the lotus feet of the Lord, the goddess of fortune, Lakṣmī, attained perfection. (7) By rendering personal service to the Lord, Hanumān attained the desired result. (8) Through his friendship with the Lord, Arjuna attained the desired result. (9) By surrendering everything that he had, Mahārāja Bali attained the desired result.

Actually, the explanation of this *mantra* and of practically all the *mantras* of the Vedic hymns is summarized in the *Vedānta-sūtras* and properly explained in *Śrīmad-Bhāgavatam*. *Śrīmad-Bhāgavatam* is the mature fruit of the Vedic tree of wisdom. In *Śrīmad-Bhāgavatam* this particular *mantra* is explained in the questions and answers between Mahārāja Parīkṣit and Śukadeva Gosvāmī at the very beginning of their meeting. Hearing and chanting of the science of God is the basic principle of devotional life. The complete

Bhāgavatam was heard by Mahārāja Parīkṣit and chanted by Śukadeva Gosvāmī. Mahārāja Parīkṣit inquired from Śukadeva because Śukadeva was a greater spiritual master than any great *yogī* or transcendentalist of his time.

Mahārāja Parīkṣit's main question was, "What is the duty of every man, specifically at the time of death?" Śukadeva Gosvāmī answered,

tasmād bhārata sarvātmā
bhagavān īśvaro hariḥ
śrotavyaḥ kīrtitavyaś ca
smartavyaś cecchatābhayam

"Everyone who is desirous of being free from all anxieties should always hear about, glorify, and remember the Personality of Godhead, who is the supreme director of everything, the extinguisher of all difficulties, and the Supersoul of all living entities." (*Bhāg.* 2.1.5)

So-called human society is generally engaged at night in sleeping and having sex and during the daytime in earning as much money as possible or else in shopping for family maintenance. People have very little time to talk about the Personality of Godhead or to inquire about Him. They have dismissed God's existence in so many ways, primarily by declaring Him to be impersonal, that is, without sense perception. However, in Vedic literature—whether the *Upaniṣads*, *Vedānta-sūtras*, *Bhagavad-gītā*, or *Śrīmad-Bhāgavatam*—it is declared that the Lord is a sentient being and is supreme over all other living entities. His glorious activities are identical with Himself. One should therefore not indulge in hearing and speaking of the activities of worldly politicians and so-called big men in society—activities that are all rubbish—but should mold his life in such a way that he can engage in godly activities without wasting a second.

Śrī Īśopaniṣad directs us toward such godly activities.

Unless one is accustomed to devotional practice, what will he remember at the time of death when the body is dislocated, and how can he pray to the almighty Lord to remember his sacrifices? Sacrifice means denying the interest of the senses. One has to learn this art by employing the senses in the service of the Lord during one's lifetime. One can utilize the results of such practice at the time of death.

MANTRA EIGHTEEN

अग्ने नय सुपथा राये अस्मान् विश्वानि देव वयुनानि विद्वान् ।
युयोध्यस्मज्जुहुराणमेनो भूयिष्ठां ते नमउक्तिं विधेम ॥१८॥

agne naya supathā rāye asmān
viśvāni deva vayunāni vidvān
yuyodhy asmaj juhurāṇam eno
bhūyiṣṭhāṁ te nama uktiṁ vidhema

agne—O my Lord, powerful like the fire; *naya*—kindly lead; *supathā*—by the right path; *rāye*—for reaching You; *asmān*—us; *viśvāni*—all; *deva*—O my Lord; *vayunāni*—actions; *vidvān*—the knower; *yuyodhi*—kindly remove; *asmat*—from us; *juhurāṇam*—all hindrances on the path; *enaḥ*—all vices; *bhūyiṣṭhām*—most numerous; *te*—unto You; *namaḥ utkim*—words of obeisance; *vidhema*—I do.

TRANSLATION

O my Lord, powerful as fire, omnipotent one, now I offer You all obeisances and fall on the ground at Your feet. O my Lord, please lead me on the right path to reach You, and since You know all that I have done in the past, please free me from the reactions to my past sins, so that there will be no hindrance to my progress.

PURPORT

By surrendering and praying for the causeless mercy of the Lord, the devotee can progress on the path of complete self-realization. The Lord is addressed as fire because He can burn anything into ashes, including the sins of the surrendered soul. As described in the previous *mantras*, the real or ultimate aspect of the Absolute is His feature as the Personality of Godhead. His impersonal *brahmajyoti* feature is a dazzling covering over His face. Fruitive activities, or the *karma-kāṇḍa* path of self-realization, is the lowest stage in this endeavor. As soon as such activities even slightly deviate from the regulative principles of the *Vedas*, they are transformed into *vikarma*, or acts against the interest of the actor. Such *vikarma* is enacted by the illusioned living entity simply for sense gratification, and thus such activities become hindrances on the path of self-realization.

Self-realization is possible in the human form of life, but not in other forms. There are 8,400,000 species or forms of life, of which the human form, qualified by brahminical culture, presents the only chance to obtain knowledge of transcendence. Brahminical culture includes truthfulness, sense control, forbearance, simplicity, full knowledge, and full faith in God. It is not that one simply becomes proud of his high parentage. To be a son of a *brāhmaṇa* is a chance to become a *brāhmaṇa*, just as being the son of a big man affords one a chance to become a big man. However, such a birthright is not everything, for one still has to attain the brahminical qualifications for himself. As soon as one becomes proud of his birth as the son of a *brāhmaṇa* and neglects to acquire the qualifications of a real *brāhmaṇa*, he at once becomes degraded and falls from the path of self-realization. Thus his life mission as a human being is defeated.

In *Bhagavad-gītā* (6.41–42) we are assured by the Lord that the *yoga-bhraṣṭas*, or souls fallen from the path of self-realization, are given a chance to rectify themselves by taking birth either in the families of good *brāhmaṇas* or in the families of rich merchants. Such births afford higher chances for self-realization. If these chances are misused due to illusion, one loses the good opportunity of human life afforded by the almighty Lord.

The regulative principles are such that one who follows them is promoted from the platform of fruitive activities to the platform of transcendental knowledge. After many, many births, and after attaining the platform of transcendental knowledge, one becomes perfect when he surrenders unto the Lord. This is the general procedure. But one who surrenders at the very beginning, as recommended in this *mantra*, at once surpasses all stages simply by adopting the devotional attitude. As stated in *Bhagavad-gītā* (18.66), the Lord at once takes charge of such a surrendered soul and frees him from the reactions to his sinful acts. There are many sinful reactions involved in *karma-kāṇḍa* activities, and in *jñāna-kāṇḍa*, the path of philosophical development, the number of such sinful activities is less. However, in devotional service to the Lord, the path of *bhakti*, there is practically no chance of incurring sinful reactions. One who is a devotee of the Lord attains all the good qualifications of the Lord Himself, what to speak of the qualifications of a *brāhmaṇa*. A devotee automatically attains the qualifications of an expert *brāhmaṇa* authorized to perform sacrifices, even though the devotee may not have taken his birth in a *brāhmaṇa* family. Such is the omnipotence of the Lord. He can make a man born in a *brāhmaṇa* family as degraded as a lowborn dog-eater, and he can also make a lowborn dog-eater superior to a qualified *brāhmaṇa* simply on the strength of devotional service.

Since the omnipotent Lord is situated within the heart of everyone, He can give directions to His sincere devotees by which they can attain the right path. Such directions are especially offered to the devotee even if he desires something else. As far as others are concerned, God gives sanction to the doer only at the risk of the doer. In the case of a devotee, however, the Lord directs him in such a way that he never acts wrongly. In *Śrīmad-Bhāgavatam* (11.5.42) it is said,

sva-pāda-mūlaṁ bhajataḥ priyasya
tyaktānya-bhāvasya hariḥ pareśaḥ
vikarma yac cotpatitaṁ kathañcid
dhunoti sarvaṁ hṛdi sanniviṣṭaḥ

"The Lord is so kind to His devotee that even though the devotee sometimes falls into the entanglement of *vikarma*—acts against the Vedic directions—the Lord at once rectifies the mistakes within the heart of a devotee. This is because the devotees are very dear to the Lord."

In this *mantra* the devotee prays to the Lord to rectify him from within his heart. To err is human. A conditioned soul is very often apt to commit mistakes, and the only remedial measure to take against such unknown sins is to give oneself up to the lotus feet of the Lord so that He may guide. The Lord takes charge of fully surrendered souls; thus all problems are solved simply by surrendering oneself unto the Lord and acting in terms of the Lord's directions. Such directions are given to the sincere devotee in two ways. One is by way of the saints, scriptures, and spiritual master; and the other is by way of the Lord Himself, who resides within the heart of everyone. Thus the devotee is protected in all respects.

Vedic knowledge is transcendental and cannot be understood by mundane educational procedures. One can understand the Vedic *mantras* only by the grace of the Lord and the spiritual master. If one takes shelter of a bona fide spiritual master, it is to be understood that he has obtained the grace of the Lord. The Lord appears as the spiritual master for the devotee. Thus the spiritual master, the Vedic injunctions, and the Lord Himself from within all guide the devotee in full strength. Thus there is no chance for a devotee to fall again into the *māyā* of material illusion. The devotee, thus protected all around, is sure to reach the ultimate destination of perfection. The entire process is hinted at in this *mantra*, and *Śrīmad-Bhāgavatam* (1.2.17–20) explains it further.

Hearing and chanting of the glories of the Lord are in themselves acts of piety. The Lord wants everyone to hear and chant because He is the well-wisher of all living entities. By hearing and chanting of the glories of the Lord, one becomes cleansed of all undesirable things, and his devotion becomes fixed upon the Lord. At this stage the devotee acquires the brahminical qualifications, and the resultant reactions of the lower modes of nature (passion and ignorance) completely vanish. The devotee becomes fully enlightened by virtue of his devotional service, and thus he comes to know the path of the Lord and the way to attain Him. As all doubts diminish, one becomes a pure devotee.

Thus end the Bhaktivedanta purports of Śrī Īśopaniṣad, *the knowledge that brings one nearer to the Supreme Personality of Godhead, Kṛṣṇa.*

About the Author

His Divine Grace A. C. Bhaktivedanta Swami Prabhupāda appeared in this world in 1896 in Calcutta, India. He first met his spiritual master, Śrīla Bhaktisiddhānta Sarasvatī Gosvāmī, in Calcutta in 1922. Bhaktisiddhānta Sarasvatī, a prominent religious scholar and the founder of sixty-four Gauḍīya Maṭhas (Vedic institutes), liked this educated young man and convinced him to dedicate his life to teaching Vedic knowledge. Śrīla Prabhupāda became his student, and eleven years later (1933) at Allahabad he became his formally initiated disciple.

At their first meeting, in 1922, Śrīla Bhaktisiddhānta Sarasvatī Ṭhākura requested Śrīla Prabhupāda to broadcast Vedic knowledge through the English language. In the years that followed, Śrīla Prabhupāda wrote a commentary on the *Bhagavad-gītā*, assisted the Gauḍīya Maṭha in its work and, in 1944, without assistance, started *Back to Godhead*, an English fortnightly magazine, edited it, typed the manuscripts and checked the galley proofs. He even distributed the individual copies and struggled to maintain the publication. Once begun, the magazine never stopped; it is now being continued by his disciples in the West and is published in over thirty languages.

Recognizing Śrīla Prabhupāda's philosophical learning and devotion, the Gauḍīya Vaiṣṇava Society honored him in 1947 with the title "Bhaktivedanta." In 1950, at the age of fifty-four, Śrīla Prabhupāda retired from married life, adopting the *vānaprastha* (retired) order to devote more time to his studies and writing. Śrīla Prabhupāda traveled to the holy city of Vṛndāvana, where he lived in very humble circumstances in the historic medieval temple of Rādhā-Dāmodara. There he engaged for several years in deep study and writing. He accepted the renounced order of life (*sannyāsa*) in 1959. At Rādhā-Dāmodara, Śrīla Prabhupāda began work on his life's masterpiece: a multivolume translation of and commentary on the eighteen-thousand-verse *Śrīmad-Bhāgavatam* (*Bhāgavata Purāṇa*). He also wrote *Easy Journey to Other Planets.*

After publishing three volumes of the *Bhāgavatam*, Śrīla Prabhupāda came to the United States, in 1965, to fulfill the mission of his spiritual master. Subsequently, His Divine Grace wrote more than sixty volumes of authoritative translations, commentaries and summary studies of the philosophical and religious classics of India.

In 1965, when he first arrived by freighter in New York City, Śrīla Prabhupāda was practically penniless. It was after almost a year of great difficulty that he established the International Society for Krishna Consciousness in July of 1966. Before his passing away on November 14, 1977, he guided the Society and saw it grow to a worldwide confederation of more than one hundred *āśramas*, schools, temples, institutes and farm communities.

In 1968, Śrīla Prabhupāda created New Vrindaban, an experimental Vedic community in the hills of West Virginia. Inspired by the success of New Vrindaban, now a thriving farm community of more than two thousand acres, his students have since founded several similar communities in the United States and abroad.

In 1972, His Divine Grace introduced the Vedic system of primary and secondary education in the West by founding the Gurukula school in Dallas, Texas. Since then, under his supervision, his disciples have established children's schools throughout the United States and the rest of the world, with the principal educational center now located in Vṛndāvana, India.

Śrīla Prabhupāda also inspired the construction of several large international cultural centers in India. The center at Śrīdhāma Māyāpur in West Bengal is the site for a planned spiritual city, an ambitious project for which construction will extend over the next decade. In Vṛndāvana, India, is the magnificent Kṛṣṇa-Balarāma Temple and International Guesthouse. There is also a major cultural and educational center in Bombay. Other centers are planned in a dozen other important locations on the Indian subcontinent.

Śrīla Prabhupāda's most significant contribution, however, is his books. Highly respected by the academic community for their authoritativeness, depth and clarity, they are used as standard textbooks in numerous college courses. His writings have been translated into over thirty languages. The Bhaktivedanta Book Trust, established in 1972 exclusively to publish the works of His Divine Grace, has thus become the world's largest publisher of books in the field of Indian religion and philosophy.

In just twelve years, in spite of his advanced age, Śrīla Prabhupāda circled the globe fourteen times on lecture tours that took him to six continents. In spite of such a vigorous schedule, Śrīla Prabhupāda continued to write prolifically. His writings constitute a veritable library of Vedic philosophy, religion, literature and culture.

Glossary

A

Ācārya—a spiritual master; one who teaches by example.

Adhīra—one who has not undergone the training of a *dhīra*.

Akarma—action that frees one from the cycle of birth and death.

Amara—deathless.

Ānanda—the Supreme Lord's aspect of bliss.

Ananta—unlimited.

Anumāna—inductive knowledge.

Apāpa-viddha—pure and uncontaminated.

Aparā prakṛti—the inferior energy of the Lord.

Apauruṣeya—not delivered by any mundane person.

Arcā-vigraha—the worshipable form of the Lord.

Āroha—the ascending process of knowledge.

Asura—a demon.

Ātmā—the soul.

Ātma-hā—a killer of the soul.

Avidyā—ignorance.

Avyakta—the unmanifested stage of creation.

B

Bhagavān—the possessor of all opulences.

Bhaktas—devotees of Śrī Kṛṣṇa.

Brahmajyoti—the effulgence emanating from the body of the Supreme Lord, which illuminates the spiritual world.

Brāhmaṇas—the intelligent class of men who know what is Brahman.

Buddha—learned.

C

Cit—the Supreme Lord's aspect of knowledge.

D

Dhīra—one who is not disturbed by material illusion.

Dvija-bandhu—one born in a *brāhmaṇa* family but not qualified as a *brāhmaṇa.*

G

Guru—a spiritual master.

I

Īśāvāsya—the God-centered conception.

J

Jīva-śakti—the living force.

Jñāna—the culture of knowledge.

K

Kaniṣṭha-adhikārī—a person in the lowest stage of realization of God.

Karma—action performed in terms of one's prescribed duties, as mentioned in revealed scriptures.

Karma-bandhana—work that binds one to the material world.

Karma-yoga—offering the fruit of one's work to Kṛṣṇa.

Karmīs—those engaged in activities of sense gratification.

Kṣatriyas—the administrator group in society.

M

Madhyama-adhikārīs—those who have attained the intermediate stage of God realization.

Mahā-bhāgavata—a great personality who sees everything in relation to the Supreme Lord.

Māyā—illusion; accepting something that is not.
Māyayāpahṛta-jñānīs—those who believe that they themselves are God.
Mṛtyuloka—the place of death, the material world.
Mūḍhas—fools or asses.

N

Naiṣkarma—*See: Akarma*
Narādhama—the lowest of human beings.
Nirguṇa—without material qualities.

P

Param Brahma—the supreme spirit.
Paramparā—the line of disciplic succession.
Parā prakṛti—the superior energy of the Lord.
Parā śakti—*See: Parā prakṛti*
Pitās—forefathers.
Prāṇa-vāyu—the movements of different kinds of airs in the body.
Prasāda—food spiritualized by being offered to Kṛṣṇa.
Pratyakṣa—direct evidence.

S

Sac-cid-ānanda-vigraha—eternal, knowing, and blissful—in full form.
Saguṇa—with qualities.
Sat—the Supreme Lord's aspect of eternity.
Śrīmat—a *vaiśya;* a member of the mercantile community.
Śruti—knowledge acquired by hearing.
Śuci—a spiritually advanced *brāhmaṇa.*
Śuddha—antiseptic.
Śūdras—the worker class in society.
Śukra—omnipotent.
Sura—a godly person.

T

Tri-pād-vibhūti—the spiritual nature, which is three fourths of the Lord's energy.

U

Uttama-adhikārī—a person in the highest stage of God-realization.

V

Vaikuṇṭhalokas—the planets in the spiritual sky.
Vaiśyas—the mercantile group in society.
Varṇāśrama—the four divisions of society and four divisions of spiritual life.
Veda—knowledge.
Vedas—the original revealed scriptures, first spoken by the Lord Himself.
Veda-vāda-ratas—those who give their own explanations of the *Vedas.*
Vidyā—knowledge.
Vikarma—action performed by the misuse of one's freedom.
Viṣṇu-tattva—a plenary portion of the Supreme Lord.

Y

Yoga-bhraṣṭa—a soul fallen from the path of self-realization.

Sanskrit Pronunciation Guide

Throughout the centuries, the Sanskrit language has been written in a variety of alphabets. The mode of writing most widely used throughout India, however, is called *devanāgarī*, which means, literally, the writing used in "the cities of the demigods." The *devanāgarī* alphabet consists of forty-eight characters: thirteen vowels and thirty-five consonants. Ancient Sanskrit grammarians arranged this alphabet according to practical linguistic principles, and this order has been accepted by all Western scholars. The system of transliteration used in this book conforms to a system that scholars in the last fifty years have accepted to indicate the pronunciation of each Sanskrit sound.

Vowels

अ a आ ā इ i ई ī उ u ऊ ū ऋ ṛ
ॠ ṝ ऌ ḷ ए e ऐ ai ओ o औ au

Consonants

Gutturals:	क ka	ख kha	ग ga	घ gha	ङ ṅa
Palatals:	च ca	छ cha	ज ja	झ jha	ञ ña
Cerebrals:	ट ṭa	ठ ṭha	ड ḍa	ढ ḍha	ण ṇa
Dentals:	त ta	थ tha	द da	ध dha	न na
Labials:	प pa	फ pha	ब ba	भ bha	म ma
Semivowels:	य ya	र ra	ल la	व va	
Sibilants:	श śa	ष ṣa	स sa		
Aspirate:	ह ha	Anusvāra: ं ṁ	Visarga: ः ḥ		

Numerals

० -0 १-1 २-2 ३-3 ४-4 ५-5 ६-6 ७-7 ८-8 ९-9

The vowels are written as follows after a consonant:

ा ā ि i ी ī ु u ू ū ृ ṛ ॄ ṝ े e ै ai ो o ौ au

For example: क ka का kā कि ki की kī कु ku कू kū

कृ kṛ कॄ kṝ के ke कै kai को ko कौ kau

Generally two or more consonants in conjunction are written together in a special form, as for example: क्ष kṣa त्र tra

The vowel "**a**" is implied after a consonant with no vowel symbol.

The symbol virāma (्) indicates that there is no final vowel: क्

The vowels are pronounced as follows:

a — as in but
ā — as in far but held twice as long as **a**
ai — as in **ai**sle
au — as in h**ow**
e — as in th**ey**
i — as in p**i**n
ī — as in p**i**que but held twice as long as **i**
l̥ — as in **lree**
o — as in **go**
ṛ — as in **ri**m
ṝ — as in **ree**d but held twice as long as **ṛ**
u — as in p**u**sh
ū — as in r**u**le but held twice as long as **u**

The consonants are pronounced as follows:

Gutturals
(pronounced from the throat)
k — as in **k**ite
kh — as in Ec**kh**art
g — as in **g**ive
gh — as in di**g-h**ard
ṅ — as in si**ng**

Labials
(pronounced with the lips)
p — as in **p**ine
ph — as in u**p-h**ill (not **f**)
b — as in **b**ird
bh — as in ru**b-h**ard
m — as in **m**other

Cerebrals
(pronounced with tip of tongue against roof of mouth)
ṭ — as in tub
ṭh — as in light-heart
ḍ — as in dove
ḍh — as in red-hot
ṇ — as in sing

Dentals
(pronounced as cerebrals but with tongue against teeth)
t — as in tub
th — as in light-heart
d — as in dove
dh — as in red-hot
n — as in nut

Aspirate
h — as in home

Anusvāra
ṁ — a resonant nasal sound like in the French word *bon*

Palatals
(pronounced with middle of tongue against palate)
c — as in chair
ch — as in staunch-heart
j — as in joy
jh — as in hedgehog
ñ — as in canyon

Semivowels
y — as in yes
r — as in run
l — as in light
v — as in vine, except when preceded in the same syllable by a consonant, then like in swan

Sibilants
ś — as in the German word *sprechen*
ṣ — as in shine
s — as in sun

Visarga
ḥ — a final **h**-sound: **aḥ** is pronounced like **aha**; **iḥ** like **ihi**

There is no strong accentuation of syllables in Sanskrit, or pausing between words in a line, only a flowing of short and long (twice as long as the short) syllables. A long syllable is one whose vowel is long (**ā, ai, au, e, ī, o, ṝ, ū**) or whose short vowel is followed by more than one consonant (including **ḥ** and **ṁ**). Aspirated consonants (consonants followed by an **h**) count as single consonants.

Index of Sanskrit Verses

This index constitutes a complete listing of all lines of each of the Sanskrit verses of *Śrī Īśopaniṣad*, arranged in English alphabetical order. In the first column the Sanskrit transliteration is given, and in the second and third columns respectively the *mantra* number and page number for each verse are to be found.

agne naya supathā rāye asmān	18	107
andhaṁ tamaḥ praviśanti	9	43
andhaṁ tamaḥ praviśanti	12	63
andhena tamasāvṛtāḥ	3	15
anejad ekaṁ manaso javīyo	4	19
anyad āhur asambhavāt	13	69
anyad āhur avidyayā	10	49
anyad evāhuḥ sambhavād	13	69
anyad evāhur vidyayā	10	49
asnāviraṁ śuddham apāpa-viddham	8	37
asuryā nāma te lokā	3	15
athedaṁ bhasmāntaṁ śarīram	17	97
ātmaivābhūd vijānataḥ	7	33
ātmany evānupaśyati	6	29
avidyayā mṛtyuṁ tīrtvā	11	55
bhūyiṣṭhāṁ te nama uktiṁ vidhema	18	107
ekatvam anupaśyataḥ	7	33
evaṁ tvayi nānyatheto 'sti	2	11
hiraṇmayena pātreṇa	15	85
īśāvāsyam idaṁ sarvaṁ	1	5
iti śuśruma dhīrāṇāṁ	10	49
iti śuśruma dhīrāṇāṁ	13	69
jijīviṣec chataṁ samāḥ	2	11
kavir manīṣī paribhūḥ svayambhūr	8	37
krato smara kṛtaṁ smara	17	97
kurvann eveha karmāṇi	2	11
mā gṛdhaḥ kasya svid dhanam	1	5
nainad devā āpnuvan pūrvam arṣat	4	19
na karma lipyate nare	2	11
oṁ krato smara kṛtaṁ smara	17	97
oṁ pūrṇam adaḥ pūrṇam idaṁ	Inv.	1
pūrṇam evāvaśiṣyate	Inv.	1
pūrṇasya pūrṇam ādāya	Inv.	1
pūrṇāt pūrṇam udacyate	Inv.	1
pūṣann ekarṣe yama sūrya prājāpatya	16	91

sambhūtiṁ ca vināśaṁ ca	14	79
sambhūtyāmṛtam aśnute	14	79
sa paryagāc chukram akāyam avraṇam	8	37
sarva-bhūteṣu cātmānaṁ	6	29
satya-dharmāyā dṛṣṭaye	15	85
satyasyāpihitaṁ mukham	15	85
tad antarasya sarvasya	5	23
tad dhāvato 'nyān atyeti tiṣṭhat	4	19
tad dūre tad v antike	5	23
tad ejati tan naijati	5	23
tad u sarvasyāsya bāhyataḥ	5	23
tad vedobhayaṁ saha	11	55
tāṁs te pretyābhigacchanti	3	15
tasminn apo mātariśvā dadhāti	4	19
tato bhūya iva te tamo	9	43
tato bhūya iva te tamo	12	63
tato na vijugupsate	6	29
tatra ko mohaḥ kaḥ śoka	7	33
tat tvaṁ pūṣann apāvṛṇu	15	85
tejo yat te rūpaṁ kalyāṇatamaṁ tat te paśyāmi	16	91
tena tyaktena bhuñjīthā	1	5
vāyur anilam amṛtam	17	97
vidyāṁ cāvidyāṁ ca yas	11	55
vidyayāmṛtam aśnute	11	55
vināśena mṛtyuṁ tīrtvā	14	79
viśvāni deva vayunāni vidvān	18	107
yasmin sarvāṇi bhūtāny	7	33
yas tad vedobhayaṁ saha	14	79
yas tu sarvāṇi bhūtāny	6	29
yāthātathyato 'rthān vyadadhāc chāśvatībhyaḥ samābhyaḥ	8	37
yat kiñca jagatyāṁ jagat	1	5
ya u sambhūtyāṁ ratāḥ	12	63
ya u vidyāyāṁ ratāḥ	9	43
ye ke cātma-hano janāḥ	3	15
ye nas tad vicacakṣire	10	49
ye nas tad vicacakṣire	13	69
ye 'sambhūtim upāsate	12	63
ye 'vidyām upāsate	9	43
yo 'sāv asau puruṣaḥ so 'ham asmi	16	91
yuyodhy asmaj juhurāṇam eno	18	107

General Index

Numerals in boldface type indicate references to translations of the verses of *Śrī Īśopaniṣad.*

A

Abhijña defined, 74
Ābrahma-bhuvanāl lokāḥ
verse quoted, 66
Absolute Truth
accessibility of, 20
Brahman as, *xiii*
as consciousness, *xiii*
mental speculator's conception of, 64–65
mind can't reach, 20
nature of, *xiii*
as personal, 2, 20, 65
Personality of Godhead as, 2
realization of
via *Bhagavad-gītā*, 60
devotees attain, 93
effulgence of Lord bypassed for, **85**, 88
stages of, 2, 64–65, 86
Ācārya. See: Spiritual master(s)
Action. *See: Akarma; Karma; Vikarma;* Work
Adhīra defined, 54
Ādityas, 72
Agha demon, 87
Aham ādir hi devānām
verse quoted, 64
Akarma, 12, 13
See also: Naiṣkarma; Vikarma
Akrūra, 103
Altruism, 13, 14, 44, 68
Amara defined, 56
Analogies
boat & human body, 16
breezes & human body's facilities, 16
coconut & universe, 66
Analogies (*continued*)
decoration on dead body & misused education, 45
dreams & life's activities, 101
fever & sense gratification, 59
fire & Lord, 7, 20, 34, **107**, 108
funeral & civilization, 45
hand & living entity, 3
heat and light & Lord's potencies, 20, 27
jewel on cobra & godless education, 45
mother & *śruti, vii*
mother & *Vedas, vii*
ocean & material world, 16
root & soul, 75
salt in drop & living entities, 34
salt in ocean & Lord, 34
spaceships & planets, 52
sparks of fire & living entities, 34
sun & living entity, **79**
sun & Lord, 42, **91**
sun's rays & Brahman, 26
Ānanda defined, 2
Ananta defined, *xi*
Ānandamayo 'bhyāsāt
quoted, 87
Animals
human life compared with, 8–9 15, 16–17, 101
killing of, 8–9, 75
Antaryāmī defined, 27
Anumāna defined, *viii*
Aparā prakṛti, 6, 7, 81
Apāpa-viddham defined, 41
Apauruṣeya defined, 6
Arcā-vigraha. See: Deity of Supreme Lord

Arjuna
- *Bhagavad-gītā* heard by, 71–72, 74
- as perfect disciple, 54
- perfection attained by, 103

Āroha defined, *x*
Asambhūti defined, 63
Asuras, characteristics of, 16–18
Atharva Veda
- as division of *Vedas*, *xi*
- quoted on Lord as creator, 72

Athavā bahunaitena
- verse quoted, 86

Atheism, cult of, 67
Atheists
- activities of, 67
- Deity not understood by, 25
- devotee avoids, 30

Ātmā. *See:* Soul
Ātma-bhūta interest, 36
Ātma-hā defined, 16
Avidyā defined, 58, 81
- *See also:* Ignorance; Nescience, culture of

Avyakta defined, 82

B

Baka demon, 87
Baladeva, Lord, 39
Baladeva Vidyābhūṣaṇa, *xii*
Bali Mahārāja, 103
Bhagavad-gītā
- *See also: Bhagavad-gītā* cited; *Bhagavad-gītā*, quotations from
- Absolute Truth realized via, 61
- Arjuna receiver of, 71–72, 74
- devotional service via, 60
- interpreters of, 71–72, 83
- Lord speaker of, 32
- as *Upaniṣads'* essence, 13, 22, 76
- Vyāsadeva recorder of, 31

Bhagavad-gītā As It Is, *ix*
Bhagavad-gītā cited
- on Absolute Truth, 86
- on *akarma*, 12, 13
- on Arjuna hearing *Gītā*, 71
- on *asuras*, 18
- on birth-death cycle, 13
- on *brahma-bhūta*, 36
- on *brahmajyoti's* source, 89
- on Brahmā's life span, 56
- on demigod worship, 65, 67, 72
- on devotee aided by Lord, 77
- on devotee's behavior, 42
- on devotee's relationship with Lord, 25
- on devotional service, 82
- on disciplic succession, *viii*
- on elements of material nature, 6
- on energy of Lord, 81
- on faith in Lord, 73
- on food offered to Lord, 9
- on impersonalist's labor, 102
- on *karma*, 12
- on *karma-yoga*, 14
- on knowledge, cultivation of, 49–51
- on knowledge of Lord, 21
- on living entity as marginal potency, 35
- on living entity's intelligence, 40
- on Lord as creator, 72
- on Lord's advent, 24
- on Lord's consciousness, 74
- on Lord's form misunderstood, 39
- on *mahātmās*, 36
- on marginal potency of Lord, 35
- on material body's destruction, 98
- on material creation's maintenance, 88
- on nature pacified, 83
- on pseudoreligionist's destination, 68
- on self-realization, 17, 109

Bhagavad-gītā cited (*continued*)
on sense gratification, 44
on spiritual sky, 24
on surrender to Lord, 35, 72, 83, 109
on transcendentalists, 90
on *uttama-adhikārī*, 31
on *Vedas'* goal, 45
on Vedic knowledge, *viii*
on *vikarma*, 12
on worship, types of, 70
Bhagavad-gītā, quotations from
on Brahman's basis, 86
on devotee's relationship with Lord, 101
on demigods' source, 64
on disciplic succession, 71
on material world's miseries, 66
on surrender to Lord, 101
on transmigration via mind, 100–101
on universe supported by Lord, 86
on *varṇāśrama*, *vi*
Bhagavān
defined, 93
realization of, 86
See also: Kṛṣṇa, Lord; Personality of Godhead; Supreme Lord
Bhagavat-sandarbha, quoted on Absolute Truth, 93
Bhāgavata school, 24
Bhaktas. See: Devotees of Supreme Lord
Bhakti-rasāmṛta-sindhu, 61
Bhakti-yoga, 71, 91
See also: Devotional service
Bhaktivinoda Ṭhākura, Śrīla
cited on mundane knowledge, 51
quoted on devotee's "imperfections," 102
Birth-death cycle
causes of, 12, 52, 58, 82–83, 100–101
Birth-death cycle (*continued*)
escape from, 16, 41, **55**, 66, 83
īśāvāsya activities &, 14
karma-yoga &, 14
living entities in, 12, 52, 75
mahātmās free from, 36
science &, 80
via sense gratification, 58, 100
Brahmā, Lord
day of, 81
as first living entity, 6
Hiraṇyakaśipu &, 56
life span of, 80, 81
Lord creator of, 72
as material world's creator, 56
Nārada disciple of, 31
Vedic knowledge first received by, *viii*, 6
Brahma-bhūta interest, 36
Brahmacarya, 52
Brahmajyoti
contents of, 66
empiric philosophy leads to, 89
fall-down from, 100
impersonalists "blinded" by, 92
planets in, 65–66
realization of, 92–93
realization of Lord hindered by, **85**, **91**, 92
source of, 89, 100
See also: Brahman
Brahmaloka, 82
Brahman
as Absolute Truth, *xiii*
compared to sun's rays, 26
as *jīva-śakti's* source, 95
mental speculators reach, 64
realization of, 2, 86, 93
source of, 26, 64, 85–86, 89, 90, 95
spiritual master established in, *x*
See also: Brahmajyoti
Brāhmaṇa
defined, *vi*

Brāhmaṇa (*continued*)
qualifications of, 76, 108, 109
Brahmaṇo hi pratiṣṭhāham
verse quoted, 86
Brahma-randhra defined, 99
Brahma-saṁhitā
cited
on Absolute Truth, 20
on *brahmajyoti*, 92
on Lord as Kṛṣṇa, 73
on Lord as *sac-cid-ānanda-vigraha*, 38
on Lord within & without, 27
on mind's speed, *x*, 20
quotations from
on brahmajyoti, 89
on Kṛṣṇa's forms, *xi*
on Lord's abode, 92
on spiritual sky, *x*
Budha defined, 73

C

Caitanya, Lord, 41
Capitalists, 8
Chauvinism, 52
Cintāmaṇi-prakara-sadmasu kalpa-vṛkṣa-
verse quoted, 92
Cit defined, 2
Civilization, modern
activities of, 44, 45, 104
basis of, 35
compared to funeral, 45
education in, 44, 45
sense gratification in, 44, 59
as soul-killing, 17
Communism defined, 13
Communists, 7–8
Complete whole. *See:* Absolute Truth; Kṛṣṇa, Lord; Personality of Godhead; Supreme Lord
Conditioned souls. *See:* Souls, conditioned
Cow dung, *vii*

D

Darwin, *viii*
Dāsya defined, 88
Death, 56
See also: Birth-death cycle
Deity of Supreme Lord, 25
Demigods
Lord controller of, **19**
Lord not approachable by, **19**
Lord source of, 64
as marginal potency of Lord, 20
as nature's controllers, **19,** 20
worship to, **63,** 65, 67
worshipers of, 65, 72
Demons
Kṛṣṇa vs., 41
See also: Asuras
Devakī, *ix*, 73
Devotee(s) of Supreme Lord
Absolute Truth realized by, 93
activities of, 9, 95
Arjuna as, 71, 74
atheists avoided by, 30
brahminically qualified, 109, 111
destinations of, **91,** 94, 101, 111
human being should be, 9
"imperfections" of, 42, 102
kaniṣṭha-adhikārī as, 30
living entities purified by, 76–77
Lord directs, 110
Lord known via, *xi*, 20
Lord's relationship with, 101
madhyama-adhikārīs as, 30
vs. mental speculators, 75–76
vs. pseudo–spiritual-masters, 75
relationship with Lord, 25

Devotee(s) (*continued*)
sudurācāra appearance of, 42
uttama-adhikārī as, 31
as *yogīs*, 90
Devotional service
benefit(s) of
birth-death cycle's cessation as, 66, 83
brāhmaṇa's qualities as, 76, 109
impersonalists barred from, 102
knowledge as, 51
liberation as, 77
self-realization as, 102
sinful reaction's cessation as, 109
Vaikuṇṭha entered as, 82
via *Bhagavad-gītā*, 60
hearing & chanting as, 76, 103, 104, 111
via *Īśopaniṣad*, 90
Lord approached via, 82, 100, 109
principles of, listed, 103
See also: Worship of Supreme Lord
Dhīra, characteristics of, 53, 54
Disciple, qualifications of, 54
Disciplic succession
Lord beginning of, 6
regulative principles via, 53
Vedic knowledge via, *viii*, 6, 31–32, 70
Dvāpara-yuga, 81
Dvija-bandhu defined, *xii*

E

Earth, ages of, 81
Education, 44–45, 54
Ekatvam anupaśyataḥ quoted, 34
Energy of Supreme Lord
control of, 26

Energy of Supreme Lord (*continued*)
inferior potency of, 6, 81
marginal potency of, 20, 35
superior energy of, 6, 81, 82
Evaṁ paramparā-prāptam verse quoted, 71
Evolution, cycle of, 16, 98
External potency. *See:* Energy of Supreme Lord

F

Fire
Lord compared to, 7, 20, 34, **107**
as material element, 6
properties of, 34
Forefathers, worship of, 70
Funeral, 45

G

Gandhi, Mahatma, *v*
Garbhodakaśāyī Viṣṇu, 88
Gītopaniṣad. See: Bhagavad-gītā
God. *See:* Kṛṣṇa, Lord; Personality of Godhead; Supreme Lord
Godhead, going back to
Lord helps entities in, 41
qualifications for, 10
via Vedic literature, 57
See also: Spiritual sky
Goloka Vṛndāvana, *xi*, 92, 94
Goodness, mode of, 76
Gopīs, 41
Govardhana Hill, 41
Govinda-bhāṣya, *xii*
Govinda, Kṛṣṇa as, 73
Guru: See: Spiritual master(s)

H

Hanumān, 103
Hari-bhakti-sudhodaya, cited on education, 45
Haṭha-yoga, 87
Hindu, *vi*
Hiraṇmaya-pātra defined, 76
Hiraṇya defined, 56
Hiraṇyakaśipu, 56–57
Hospitals, 83, 84
Human being(s)
  body of, compared to boat, 16
  as devotees of Lord, 9
  facilities of, compared to breezes, 16
  laws of nature broken by, 8–10, 12
  as vegetarians, 7, 8
  See also: Human life
Humanitarianism, 13
Human life
  animal life compared with, 8–9, 15, 16, 101
  consciousness in, 3, 99, 101
  evolution to, 3, 14, 98
  karma escaped via, 12
  laws of nature benefit, 16
  purpose of, 3, 9, 18, 40, 58, 60, 75, 108
  span of, 52
Human society. *See:* Civilization, modern; Human life

I

Idol worship, 25
Ignorance
  defined, 44
  demigod worshipers in, **62**
  impersonalists in, **62**, 66–67
Ignorance (*continued*)
  "knowledge" compared with, **43–44**
  self-realization foiled by, 76
  sense gratification goal of those in, 44
  See also: Nescience, culture of
Illusion
  civilization in, 35
  defined, *v*
  devotee's protection against, 111
  living entity subject to, *v*, 6
  Lord vs., 47
  sense enjoyment as, 3
Immortality, qualifications for gaining, **55**
Impersonalists
  activities of, 102
  atheists supported by, 66
  brahmajyoti "blinds," 92
  devotional service rejected by, 102
  in ignorance, **62**, 66–67
  liberation as conceived of by, 41
  Lord's abode not realized by, 92
  personal feature of Lord rejected by, 24
  pseudoreligionists led by, 66–67
  Śaṅkarācārya leader of, *ix*
India, 45, 59
Indra, Lord, 72
Intelligence
  as material element, 6
  mind compared with, 45
  soul compared with, 45
Internal potency. *See:* Energy of Supreme Lord
Īśāvāsya
  asuras ignorant of, 18
  defined, 13
Īśopaniṣad, Śrī, contents of, 6, 93
Ittham satām brahma-sukhānubhūtyā verse quoted, 87

J

Janmādy asya yataḥ
quoted, *xiii*
Jīva defined, 90
Jīva Gosvāmī, 93
Jīva-śakti defined, 95
Jñāna defined, 82
Jñāna-kāṇḍa defined, 109
Jñānīs
destination of, 82
yogīs compared with, 90

K

Kali-yuga, *xi*, 81
Kaniṣṭha-adhikārī defined, 30, 39
Kāraṇodakaśāyī Viṣṇu, 89
Karma
bodies generated via, 75
defined, 12, 75
freedom from, **11**, 12–13
living entities rewarded via, 40
work that escapes, 10, 12–13
See also: Work
Karma-bandhana defined, 12, 13
Karma-kāṇḍa defined, 108
Karma-phala defined, 27
Karma-yoga defined, 14
Karmīs, 44, 82
Kaśipu defined, 56
Kaṭha Upaniṣad
cited on knowing the Lord, 95
cited on spiritual master, 46
Kennedy, President John F., *v*
Kingdom of God. *See:* Spiritual nature; Supreme Lord, abode of
Knowledge
via *Bhakti-rasāmṛta-sindhu*, 61
dangers of, **43–44**
deductive system of, *x*
Knowledge (*continued*)
inductive system of, *x*
knowing Lord as, 22
liberation via, 68
material, defined, *viii*
misuse of, 51–52
via *Nectar of Devotion*, 61
perfection of, 99–100
processes for cultivating, 49–52, 61
via regulative principles, 53, 109
results of those engaged in culture of, **49–52**
transcendental. *See:* Transcendental knowledge
Veda origin of, *v*, 46
Vedic. *See:* Vedic knowledge
Kṛṣṇa, Lord
advent of, 41
as Brahman's basis, 89
as butter thief, 87
Caitanya worshiped, 41
as charioteer, *xi*
demons killed by, 41, 87
Devakī mother of, *ix*, 73
devotees of. *See:* Devotees of Supreme Lord
expansions of, 39
father of, *ix*, 73
form of, *xi*, 39
gopīs danced with, 41
Govardhana Hill lifted by, 41
Kṛṣṇaloka planet of, 66
Kurukṣetra battle designed by, 74
mother of, *ix*, 73
Nārāyaṇa expansion of, 72–73
pastimes of, 41, 87–88
relationships with, listed, 88
Śaṅkarācārya accepts, *ix*
spiritual nature predominated by, 82, 83
transcendentalists accept, *ix*
Vaiṣṇavas accept, *ix*
as Vāsudeva, 90

Kṛṣṇa (*continued*)
Vasudeva father of, *ix*, 73
as *Vedānta's* compiler, *xii*
Vedāntists accept, *ix*
as *Vedas'* knower, *xii*
as Vedic knowledge's source, *vii*
See also: Personality of Godhead; Supreme Lord
Kṛṣṇa consciousness movement, *ix*, *x*
Kṛṣṇaloka, 20, 66
Kṣatriya defined, *vi*
Kṣīrodakaśāyī Viṣṇu, 88
Kurukṣetra, battle of, 74

L

Lakṣmī, goddess of fortune, 103
Lakṣmīs, 92
Lakṣmī-sahasra-śata-sambhrama-sevyamānaṁ
verse quoted, 92
Laws of nature
breaking of, 8–10, 11
death via, 56
human life benefited by, 16
Lord not subject to, 26
material life via, 18
surrender to Lord surpasses, 36
work as, 12, 17
Liberation
defined, 41
via devotional service, 77
impersonalist's conception of, 41
via knowledge, 68
Life
air of, **97**, 99
number of species of, 3, 56, 108
Living entities
in birth-death cycle, 12, 52, 75
Brahmā first of, 6
compared to hand, 3
Living entities (*continued*)
compared to salt in drop, 34
compared to sparks of fire, 32–33
compared to sun, **91**
as complete units, 2
defects of, listed, *v*, 6
desires of, fulfilled by Lord, **37**, 40, 41
devotee purifies, 76–77
as enjoyers, 35
as eternal, 12
form possessed by, 98
Godhead goal of, 40
in illusion, *v*, 6
intelligence of, 40
karma awards accordingly, 40
laws of nature broken by, 8–10, 12
life struggled for by, 12
Lord origin of, 95
Lord compared with, 94, 104
as marginal energy, 19, 35
material bodies foreign to, 98
on moon, 81
as *parā prakṛti*, 5
as qualitatively one with Lord, **33–34**
quotas for, **5**, 7
species of, numbered, 3, 56, 108
as spiritual, **33**, 58–59
as parts & parcels of Lord, 3, 21, **29**, 35, 52, 58, 94
on sun, 81
as superior energy, 6
Supersoul compared with, 94
Supersoul maintainer of, 36

M

Mādhurya defined, 88
Madhvācārya, *ix*, *xii*
Madhyama-adhikārīs, characteristics of, 30

Mahā-bhāgavata, characteristics of, **29**, 34
Mahābhārata, *xii*
Mahārāja Bali, 103
Mahārāja Prahlāda, 26
Marārāja Parīkṣit, 103, 104
Mahārāja Pṛthu, 103
Mahātmā defined, 36
Mahatma Gandhi, *v*
Mām upetya tu kaunteya
  verse quoted, 66
Marginal potency of Lord. *See:* Energy of Supreme Lord
Martyaloka planetary system, 81
Material body
  identification with, 50
  karma generates, 75
  living entities foreign to, 98
  Lord's body compared with, 38–39
  material nature forms, 98
  miseries of, listed, 50, 56, 75
  sense gratification determines type of, 98–100
  as temporary, **97**, 98
  transcendental knowledge via, 59
Material energy. *See:* Energy; Energy of Supreme Lord; Material nature
Material nature
  demigods controllers of, **19**, 20
  elements of, 2, 6, 88
  laws of. *See:* Laws of nature
  Lord not affected by, 6
  Lord's body not product of, 24
  material bodies formed via, 98
  modes of. *See:* Modes of nature
  pacification of, 83
  scientists' knowledge of, 80
  transformation of, 80
Material world
  Brahmā creator of, 56
  compared to ocean, 16
  as complete, **1**, 2
Material world (*continued*)
  conflict in, 8, 35
  as dead, 53
  deities of, 72
  devastation of, 81, 82, 83
  as external potency, 20
  spiritual master not disturbed by, 70, 73–74
  spiritual sky beyond, 24
  Supersoul controller of, 94
  Supersoul maintainer of, 86, 88
  as temporary, 2
  upper planets of, 81
  See also: Material nature
Māyā. *See:* Illusion; Material nature
Māyāśritānāṁ nara-dārakeṇa
  verse quoted, 87
Māyāvāda school of philosophy, 24
Māyayāpahṛta-jñānas, characteristics of, 45, 47
Meditation. *See: Yoga*
Mental speculation
  Brahman reached by, 64
  Lord not approachable via, 20, 21
Mental speculators
  Absolute Truth as conceived of by, 64–65
  Lord not understood by, 40, 64–65
  Lord's activities ignored by, 75
  Lord's favors not understood by, 95
  Personality of Godhead not realized by, 64–65
Mind
  intelligence compared with, 45
  speed of, *x*, 20, 24
  transcendental knowledge via, 60
  transmigration of soul determined by, 100–101
Modes of nature, 13
  See also: specific modes
Mokṣa-dharma, quoted on Lord as creator, 73

Moon
  living entities on, 81
  travel to, 65, 66
Mūḍhas defined, 44, 73
Mṛtyuloka defined, 80

N

Naiṣkarma. See: Akarma
Na me viduḥ sura-gaṇāḥ
  verse quoted, 64
Nārada Muni
  as Brahmā's disciple, 31
  Vedic knowledge received by, **viii**, 31
  Vyāsadeva disciple of, *xii*, 31
Narādhama defined, 58
Nārāyaṇa, *ix*, 72, 73
Nationalism, 13, 52
Nature. *See:* Material nature
Nectar of Devotion, The, *61*
Nescience, culture of
  chauvinism caused by, 52
  destination of those engaged in, **43**, 44
  nationalism caused by, 52
  results of engaging in, **49**
  transcendental knowledge combined with, **55**
  universities centers of, 52
Nirguṇa defined, 26, 35
Nṛsiṁha, Lord
  advent of, 26–27
  Hiraṇyakaśipu vs., 57
  as Kṛṣṇa's expansion, 39
Nuclear bombs, 8

P

Parabrahman defined, 36
Paramātmā. *See:* Supersoul
Paramparā. See: Disciplic succession
Parā prakṛti defined, 6
Parā śakti. See: Energy of Supreme Lord, superior energy
Paribhūḥ defined, 41
Parīkṣit Mahārāja, 103, 104
Passion, mode of, 13, 76
Paśyati defined, 31
Personality of Godhead
  as Absolute Truth, 2
  Bhagavān as, 61, 64
  as Brahman's source, 64
  compared to fire, 20
  as complete, **1**–3, 7
  cosmic manifestation surpassed via knowledge of, **79**
  death surpassed via knowledge of, **79**
  demigods can't approach, **19**
  as demigods' controller, **19**
  as demigods' source, 64
  devotees of. *See:* Devotees of Supreme Lord
  devotional service reaches, 67–68
  emanations from, **1**–3, 6–7
  as independent, 70
  Kṛṣṇaloka abode of, 20
  mental speculators can't realize, 64
  mind's speed vs., **19**
  Nārāyaṇa as, 72, 73
  Nṛsiṁha form of, 26, 39, 57
  as perfect, **1**
  potencies of, 2, 20–21
    See also: Energy of Supreme Lord
  as proprietor of everything, 45
  realization of, 2–3, 13, 93
  as *sac-cid-ānanda-vigraha*, 2
  as sages' source, 64
  as *sambhūti*, 63
  Supersoul representation of. *See:* Supersoul

Vaikuṇṭhaloka planet of, 65
See also: Kṛṣṇa, Lord; Supreme Lord
Phenomenal world. *See:* Material nature; Material world
Planets, compared to spaceships, 52
Politicians, 53, 59, 80, 104
Prahlāda Mahārāja, 26–27
Prajāpatis, 72
Prakṛti defined, 6
Pralamba demon, 87
Prāṇa-vāyu defined, 99
Prasāda defined, 9
Pratyakṣa defined, *viii*
Pṛthu Mahārāja, 103
Pseudoreligionists, 67, 68
Purāṇas, *xii*, 46
Pūrṇam defined, 6
Pūṣan defined, 93
Pūtanā demon, 87

Q

Quotas for living entities, **5**, 7, 45

R

Rāma, Lord, 39
Rāmānujācārya, *ix*, *xii*
Rāsa dance, 35
Regulative principles, 53, 109
Reincarnation. *See:* Birth-death cycle; Transmigration of soul
Religion
misuse of, 51, 67, 68
purpose of, 45, 60, 61
See also: Devotional service; Worship of Supreme Lord
Religionists, pseudo, 67, 68
Ṛg Veda, *xi*
Rudras, 72
Rūpa Gosvāmī, 61

S

Śabda-pramāṇa defined, *viii*
Sac-cid-ānanda-vigraha defined, 2, 38
Sacrifice defined, 105
Sages
Lord source of, 64
sense gratification rejected by, 59–60
See also: Devotees of Supreme Lord; Vaiṣṇavas
Saguṇa defined, 26
Sa kāleneha mahatā
verse quoted, 71
Salvation. *See:* Liberation
Sāma Veda, *xi*
Sambhavāt defined, 72, 77
Sambhūta defined, 74, 75
Sambhūti defined, 63–64, 83
Śaṅkarācārya, *ix*, *xii*, 73
Śaṅkara-sampradāya, *ix*
Sannyāsī, Caitanya as, 41
Śānta defined, 88
Śāśvatasya ca dharmasya
verse quoted, 86
Sat defined, 2
Satya, age of, 81
Science vs. death, 56
Scientists
material nature unknown by, 80
space travel of, 65
weapons made by, 52, 56
Self-realization
benefits of, 17
birth as factor in, 109
as education's goal, 45
ignorance foils, 76
passion foils, 76
processes for progress in, 108

Self-realization (*continued*)
via regulative principles, 50
rejection of, 17, 18
via religion, 60
Self-sufficient philosopher, **37**
Sense gratification
activities of, 13
birth-death cycle caused by, 58, 99, 100
compared to fever, 59
in current civilization, 44, 59
demigods worshiped for, 65
via economic development, 60
as illusion, 3
material bodies formed via, 98, 99
material bondage caused by, 46
as pseudoreligionist's goal, 68
relief work motivated by, 84
sages reject, 59–60
transmigration of soul caused by, 100
Vedas regulate, 60
veda-vāda-rata pursue, 45, 46
vikarma enacted for, 108
via work, 13
Senses, as imperfect, *vi, viii, x,* 6, 14
Śiva, Lord, 72, 73
Slaughterhouses, 75
Socialism, 13, 14
Soul(s)
compared to root of tree, 74–75
as conditioned, *v*
intelligence compared with, 45
killer of, **15**, 16
as liberated, *v*
transmigration of. *See:* Transmigration of soul
Space travel, 64
Species, number of, 3, 56, 108
Spiritual master(s)
acceptance of, *x*, 50
brāhmaṇa's qualities obtained via, 76
Spiritual master(s) (*continued*)
cheaters pose as, 46, 68, 74, 75
qualifications of, *x*, 54, 70, 71, 73
regulative principles followed via, 53
Vedas understood via, 46
veda-vāda-ratas disobey, 46
Vedic knowledge via, 6, 70, 111
See also: Disciplic succession
Spiritual nature
body for life in, 99
Kṛṣṇa predominating personality of, 82, 83
yogīs attain, 82
See also: Brahman
Spiritual sky
as eternal, *ix*
as internal potency, 20
material universe far from, 24
as Lord's abode, 24
planets in, 82
as unlimited, *x*
See also: Supreme Lord, abode of
Śrīmad-Bhāgavatam
See also: Śrīmad-Bhāgavatam cited; *Śrīmad-Bhāgavatam,* quotations from
Parīkṣit hearer of, 103, 104
Śukadeva speaker of, 104
as *Vedānta-sūtra's* commentator, 32, 74
Vyāsadeva author of, *xiii*, 32, 89
Śrīmad-Bhāgavatam cited
on Absolute Truth, *xiii*
on devotee's destination, 111
on life's goal, 40
on Nārada instructing Vyāsadeva, *xii*
Śrīmad-Bhāgavatam, quotations from
on Brahman, 87
on devotee directed by Lord, 76,110
on devotee's activities, 61
on devotee's potency, 76
on devotional service's benefits, 104

Śrīmad-Bhāgavatam, quotations from (*continued*)
  on hearing of Lord's activities, 61, 76
  on Kṛṣṇa's cowherd pastimes, 87
Śrīmat defined, 17
Śrotavyaḥ kīrtitavyaś ca
  verse quoted, 61, 104
Śruti
  compared to mother, *vii*
  defined, *vii*, *viii*
Śuci defined, 17
Śuddham defined, 41, 42
Śūdra defined, *xii*, 101
Sudurācāra defined, 42
Śukadeva Gosvāmī
  quoted on Kṛṣṇa's pastimes, 87
  Śrīmad-Bhāgavatam spoken by, 103, 104
Śukram defined, 39
Sun
  living entities compared to, **91**, 92
  Lord compared to, 42, **91**, 92
Supersoul
  as controller of material world, 94
  Kṣīrodakaśāyī Viṣṇu as, 88
  living entity compared with, 94
  living entities maintained by, 36
  as Lord's representation, 30, 36, 64, 86, 94, 104
  as maintainer of material creation, 86, 88
  realization of, 2, 86, 93
Supreme Lord
  as *abhijña*, 74
  abode of, 24, **79**, 92
  advent of
    as Deity, 25
    purpose of, 27, 82
    scholars' conception of, 24–25
  as *antaryāmī*, 27
  as *apāpa-viddham*, 41
  arcā-vigraha form of, 25
  as beneficiary, **97**
Supreme Lord (*continued*)
  as *Bhagavad-gītā's* speaker, 32
  Bhāgavata school accepts, 24
  bodily parts of, functions of, 38–39
  as *brahmajyoti's* source, 85–86, 89, 100
  as Brahman's basis, 85–86, 95
  as cause of all causes, 73
  compared to fire, 7, 34, **107**, 108
  compared to salt in ocean, 34
  compared to sun, 42, 91
  consciousness of, 74
  as controller of universe, **5**, 6
  as creator, 72, 94
  Deity form of, 25
  devotees of. *See:* Devotees of Supreme Lord
  devotional service to. *See:* Devotional service
  disciplic succession begins with, 6
  effulgence of, **85, 91**
    See also: Brahmajyoti; Brahman
  energies of, 6, 7, 20, 22, 39, 81, 82
  as enjoyer, 35
  expansions of, 39
  face of, **85**, 108
  as far away, **23**, 24
  favors of, 95
  food accepted by, 9
  form of, 38
    See also: Deity of Supreme Lord
  vs. illusion, 47
  intelligence of, 7
  knowledge as knowing, 22
  known via devotees, 20
  Kṛṣṇa original form of, 39
  laws of nature &, 26
  living entities' desires fulfilled by, **37**, 40–41
  living entities compared with, 104
  as living entities' origin, 95
  living entities parts & parcels of, **3**, 21, **29**, 35, 52, 58, 94

Supreme Lord (*continued*)
living entities qualitatively one with, **33**, 34
mahā-bhāgavata's knowledge of, **29, 33, 37**
as maintainer of universe, **91**, 93
material nature can't affect, 6
māyayāpahṛta-jñānas' conception of, 47
mental speculators can't understand, 20, 21, 40
mind's speed vs., 20, 24
as near, **23**, 24
Nṛsiṁha form of, 26, 57
obeisances to, **91**
as omnipotent, **107**, 110
as omniscient, **37**
as owner of universe, **5**, 6
as *paribhūḥ*, 41
parts & parcels of. *See:* Living entities
personal feature of, 24, 27, 36
potencies of
categories of, 6, 20
compared to heat & light, 27
contradictions prove, 24
service accepted via, 25
See also: Energies of Supreme Lord
as *prajāpatis'* creator, 72
as primeval philosopher, **91**, 93
as proprietor of everything, 44
as pure, **37**, 42
as *pūrṇam*, 6
puruṣa incarnation of, 88
as *pūṣan*, 87
qualities of, 2, 38–39
rāsa dance of, 35
realization of
brahmajyoti hinders, **85, 91,** 92–93
stages of, 30–31, 60, 86, 89, 90
as regulating principle, **91**

Supreme Lord (*continued*)
as *sac-cid-ānanda-vigraha*, 2, 38
as self-sufficient, 41
as self-sufficient philosopher, **37**
as source of energies, 26
spiritual sky abode of, 24
as *śuddham*, 41, 42
Supersoul representation of. *See:* Supersoul
as *suras'* goal, 15–16
surrender to
benefits of, 88, 93
as knowledge's perfection, 99
laws of nature surpassed via, 36
as sustainer of all life, **85**
as uncontaminated, **37**
as unembodied, **37**, 38
universe controlled by, **5**–**8**
universe owned by, 5, 8
as universe's maintainer, **91**, 93
as Vāsudeva, 100
as Vedic knowledge's origin, 3
veins absent in, **37**
virāṭ form of, 27
walking of, **23**, 24
as within & without, **23**, 27
as witness within, 27
worshipers of. *See:* Devotees of Supreme Lord
Suras defined, 15–16
Sva-pāda-mūlaṁ bhajataḥ priyasya verse quoted, 110

T

Tad-brahma niṣkalam anantam aśeṣa-bhūtaṁ verse quoted, 89
Taṁ tam evaiti kaunteya verse quoted, 101
Tasmād bhārata sarvātmā verse quoted, 104

Tasmād ekena manasā
verse quoted, 61
Transcendentalists, *xi*, 90
See also: Devotee(s) of Supreme Lord
Transcendental knowledge
body & mind for obtaining, 59
defined, *viii*
human life meant for obtaining, 58, 59
nescience, combined with, **55**
via regulative principles, 109
Transmigration of soul
causes of, 12, 100–101
See also: Birth-death cycle
Tretā-yuga, 81
Tri-pād-vibhūti. See: Spiritual nature

U

Universe
design of, 66
devastation of, 82, 83
See also: Material world
Universities, 51, 52
Upaniṣads
Bhagavad-gītā essence of, 13, 22, 76
as Vedic literature, *xii*
Uttama-adhikārī, 30–31, 33

V

Vaikuṇṭhaloka(s), 65, 66, 82
Vaiṣṇava-sampradāya, *ix*
See also: Disciplic succession
Vaiṣṇavas. *See:* Devotees of Supreme Lord
Vaiśya defined, *vi*, 17, 101
Varāha, Lord, 39
Varāha Purāṇa, quoted on Lord as creator, 73
Varṇāśrama defined, *vi*
Vasudeva, *ix*, 73
Vāsudeva, Lord, 90, 100
Vāsudevaḥ sarvam iti
quoted, 90
Vasus, 72
Vātsalya defined, 88
Veda defined, *v*, *vi*
Vedānta xii
Vedānta-kṛd veda-vid eva cāham
quoted, *xii*
Vedānta-sūtra
quoted on Absolute Truth, *xiii*
Śrīmad-Bhāgavatam commentary of, 74
as summary of Vedic knowledge, *xii*, *xiii*
Vedāntists, *ix*
Vedas
compared to mother, *vii*
divisions of, *xi*
goal of, 45
as knowledge's origin, *v*, 46
Kṛṣṇa knower of, *xii*
sense gratification regulated via, 60
śruti as, *xii*
understood via spiritual master, 46
varṇāśrama denotes followers of, *vi*
veda-vāda-ratas' understanding of, 45, 46
Vyāsadeva compiler of, *xii*
work regulated by, 12
See also: Vedic literature
Veda-vāda-ratas, characteristics of, 45, 46
Vedavyāsa. *See:* Vyāsadeva
Vedic knowledge
acceptance of, *vii–x*
Brahmā first to receive, *viii*, 6
defined, *ix*

Vedic knowledge (*continued*)
via disciplic succession, *viii*, 6, 31–32, 70
as infallible, 6
Nārada receives, *viii*, 31
as pure, *vi*, *ix*
source of, *vii*
via spiritual master, 3, 6, 70, 94
Vedānta-sūtra summary of, *xii*, *xiii*
Vedic literature
Godhead returned to via, 57
for humans' use, 9
Mahābhārata as, *xii*
politicians' knowledge of, 80
Purāṇas as, *xii*
purpose of, 46
scientists' knowledge of, 80
Upaniṣads as, *xii*
Vyāsadeva compiler of, *xi*, *xii*
See also: Vedas
Vedic principles. *See:* Vedic knowledge
Vegetarianism, 8–9
Vidyā defined, 46
See also: Knowledge
Vidyā-rata defined, 46
Vikarma defined, 12, 108
Vikarma yac cotpatitaṁ kathañcid
verse quoted, 110
Vināśa defined, 83
Viṣṇu, Lord
energies of, 81
forms of, 88–89
Kṛṣṇa creator of, 72
Viṣṇu Purāṇa, cited on Lord's energies, 20, 81
Viṣṇusvāmī, *ix*
Viṣṇu-tattva defined, 88
Viṣṭabhyāham idaṁ kṛtsnam
verse quoted, 86
Vṛndāvana
Kṛṣṇa's pastimes in, 87–88
Vyāsadeva
Bhagavad-gītā recorded by, 32
as *Mahābhārata's* compiler, *xii*
Vyāsadeva (*continued*)
as Nārada's disciple, *xii*, 31
as *Śrīmad-Bhāgavatam's* author, *xiii*, 32, 89
as *Vedānta-sūtra's* compiler, *xii*
as *Vedas'* compiler, *xii*
as Vedic literature's compiler, *xi*, *xii*

W

Wife, attachment to, 51
Work
karma escaped via, **11**, 14
sense gratification via, 13
Vedas regulate, 12–13
See also: Karma
Worship of demigods, 72
Worship of forefathers, 70
Worship of humanity, 75
Worship of Supreme Lord
chanting as, 75
hearing as, 76
Lord's abode reached via, 70–71
result of, **69**
See also: Devotional service

Y

Yajur Veda, *xi*, 6
Yaṁ yaṁ vāpi smaran bhāvaṁ
verse quoted, 100
Yasya prabhā prabhavato jagad-aṇḍa-
verse quoted, 89
Yoga
defined, 82
goal of, 89
Yoga-bhraṣṭas defined, 109
Yogīs
destination of, 82
highest of, 90
jñānīs compared with, 90
life airs studied by, 99

An Invitation

Bhaktivedanta Manor: A gift from George Harrison

In 1973 George Harrison purchased a seventeen-acre estate outside London as a gift for the International Society for Krishna Consciousness (ISKCON).

In the past eight years, hundreds of thousands of spiritual seekers have visited this yoga *asrama,* and since 1966, millions have frequented our more than one hundred twenty meditation centers around the world to discover the ancient mysteries of *karma* and reincarnation and to understand the science of self-realization.

Every Sunday we invite you to a special open house featuring *mantra* meditation, discussions on the transcendent reality of the soul, and a free sumptuous vegetarian feast.

For more information, call or write the center nearest you.

ISKCON Centers Around the World

NORTH AMERICA

CANADA: **Edmonton, Alberta**—10132 142nd St., T5N 2N7 / (403)452-5855; **Montreal, Quebec**—1626 Pie IX Boulevard, H1V 2C5 / (514) 527-1101; **Ottawa, Ontario**—212 Somerset St. E., K1N 6V4 / (613)233-3460; **Toronto, Ontario**—243 Avenue Rd. M5R 2J6 / (416)922-5415; **Vancouver, B.C.**—5580 S.E. Marine Dr., Burnaby V5J 3G8 / (604)430-4437; **Victoria, B.C.**—4056 Rainbow St., V8X 2A9 / (604)479-0649.

FARM: **Hemingford, Quebec (New Nandagram)**—315 Backbrush Rd., RR. No. 2, J0L 1H0 / (514)247-3429.

RESTAURANTS: **Toronto**—Govinda's, 1280 Bay St. / (416)968-1313; **Vancouver**—Govinda's, 1221 Thurlow / (604)682-8154.

U.S.A.: **Atlanta, Georgia**—1287 Ponce de Leon Ave. NE 30306 / (404)378-9182; **Baltimore, Maryland**—200 Bloomsbury Ave., Catonsville 21228 / (301)788-3883; **Berkeley, California**—2334 Stuart St. 94705 / (415) 843-7874; **Boston, Massachusetts**—72 Commonwealth Ave. 02116 / (617)536-1695; **Chicago, Illinois**—1716 West Lunt Ave. 60626 / (312)973-0900; **Cleveland, Ohio**—15720 Euclid Ave., E. Cleveland 44112 / (216)851-9367; **Columbus, Ohio**—99 East 13th Ave. 43201 / (614) 299-5084. **Dallas, Texas**—5430 Gurley Ave. 75223 / (214)827-6330; **Denver, Colorado**—1400 Cherry St. 80220 / (303)333-5461; **Detroit, Michigan**—383 Lenox Ave. 48215 / (313)824-6000; **E. Lansing, Michigan**—319 Grove St. 48823 / (517)351-6603; **Gainesville, Florida**—Rt. 2, Box 24, Alachua, 32615 / (904)462-1143; **Hartford, Connecticut**—1683 Main St., East Hartford 06108 / (203)528-1600; **Honolulu, Hawaii**—51 Coelho Way 96817 / (808)595-3947; **Houston, Texas**—1111 Rosalie St. 77004 / (713)526-9860; **Laguna Beach, California**—644 S. Coast Hwy. 92651 / (714)497-3638; **Las Vegas, Nevada**—5605 Alta Dr. 87066 (702)870-6638; **Long Island, New York**—197 S. Ocean Ave., Freeport 11520 / (516)378-6184; **Los Angeles, California**—3764 Watseka Ave. 90034 / (213) 558-9016; **Miami Beach, Florida**—2445 Collins Ave. 33140 / (305)531-0331; **Monticello, New York**—P.O. Box 388, Lake Huntington 12752 / (914)932-8303; **Newark, Delaware**—168 Elkton Rd. 19711 / (302)-453-8510; **New Orleans, Louisiana**—2936 Esplanade Ave. 70119 / (504)488-7433; **New York, NY**—309 Schermerhorn St., Brooklyn 11217 / (212)246-3503; **Philadelphia, PA**—51 W. Allens Lane 19119 / (215)247-4600; **Portland, OR**—3828 S.E. Division St. 97202 / (503)231-5792; **Providence, RI**—39 Glendale Ave. 02906 / (401)273-9010; **Queens, NY**—90-28 43rd Ave., Elmhurst 11373 / (212)457-6768; **St. Louis, MO**—3926 Lindell Blvd. 63108 / (314)-535-8085; **San Diego, CA**—1030 Grand Ave., Pacific Beach 92109 / (714)483-2500; **San Francisco, CA**—1403 Willard St. 94117 / (415)753-9704; **San Juan, PR**—Box 215, Rt. 181, Gurabo, Santa Rita 00658; **Seattle, WA**—400 18th Ave. E. 98112 / (206)329-7011; **State College, PA**—103 E. Hamilton Ave. 16801 / (814)234-1867; **Tallahassee, FL**—831 W. Saint Augustine St. 32304 / (904)222-0790; **Topanga, CA**—20395 Callon Dr. 90290 / (213)455-1658; **Towaco, NJ**—100 Jacksonville Rd. (mail: P.O. Box 109, 07082) / (201)299-0970; **Washington, DC**—10310 Oaklyn Rd., Potomac, MD 20854 / (301)299-2100.

FARMS: Carriere, Mississippi (New Tālavan)—Rt. No. 2, Box 449, 39426 / (601)798-6705; **Gainesville, Florida**—contact ISKCON Gainesville; **Gurabo, Puerto Rico (New Gandhamadana)**—Box 215 B, Route 181, Santarita 00658; **Hopland, California (New Vraja-mandala Dhama)**—Route 175, Box 469, 95449 / (707)744-1100; **Hotchkiss, Colorado (New Barshana)**—P.O. Box 112, 81419 / (303)527-4584; **Lynchburg, Tennessee (Murari-sevaka)**—Rt. No. 1, Box 146-A, (Mulberry) 37359 / (615)759-7058; **Moundsville, West Virginia (New Vrindaban)**—R.D. No. 1, Box 319, Hare Krishna Ridge 26041 / (304)845-2790; **Port Royal, Pennsylvania (Gita-nāgari)**—R.D. No. 1, 17082 / (717)-527-2493.

RESTAURANTS: **Columbus, Ohio**—Simply Wonderful, 2044 High Street 43201 / (614)299-6132; **Los Angeles**—Govinda's, 9634 Venice Blvd., 90230 / (213)836-1269; **New York, New York**—Govinda's (at ISKCON New York); **St. Louis, Missouri**—(at ISKCON St. Louis) / (341)535-8161; **San Juan, Puerto Rico**—Govinda's (at ISKCON San Juan); **Washington, D.C.**—Govinda's, 515 8th St. S.E. 20003 / (202)543-9600.

EUROPE

Amsterdam, Holland—Keizersgracht 94 / 020-249 410; **Antwerp, Belgium**—25 Katelijnevest / 031-320987; **Athens, Greece**—133 Solonos; **Catania, Sicily**—Via Empedocle 84, 95100 / 095-522-252; **Copenhagen, Denmark**—Korfuvej 9, 2300 Copenhagen S / 972337; **Dublin, Ireland**—2 Belvedere Place, Dublin 1 / 743-767; **Duedingen, Switzerland**—Im Stillen Tal, CH 3186 Duedingen (FR) / (037) 43.26.97; **Gallarate, Italy**—Via A. Volta 19, Gallarate 20131 (VA) / 0331-783-268; **Göthenburg, Sweden**—Karl Gustavsgatan 19, 41125 Göthenburg / 031-110955; **Heidelberg, W. Germany**—Vrindavana, Plöck 54; **London, England (city)**—10 Soho St., London W1 / 01-437-3662; **London, England (country)**—Bhaktivedanta Manor, Letchmore Heath, Watford, Hertfordshire WD2 8EP / Radlett 7244; **Madrid, Spain**—Calle Arturo Sorio No. 209; **Munich, W. Germany**—Govinda's Club, Kaulbachstrasse 1, 8000 Munchen / 089-280807; **Paris, France**—20 rue Vieille du Temple, Paris 75004 / 500-63-58; **Rome, Italy**—Salita del Poggio Laurentino 7, Rome 00144 / (06)593-075; **Septon, Belgium**—Chateau de Petit Somme, Septon 5482 / 086-322480; **Stockholm, Sweden**—Korsnas Gård, 140 32 Grodinge / 0753-29151; **Vienna, Austria**—Govinda Kulturzentrum, Lerchenfelderstrasse 17, A-1070 Wien / (0222) 96 10 633; **West Berlin, W. Germany**—Potsdamerstrasse 70, 1 Berlin W. 30 / 030-262-1447; **Worcester, England**—Chaitanya College at Croome Court, Severn Stoke, Worcester WR8 9DW / 090 567-214; **Zürich, Switzerland**—Bergstrasse 54, 8032 Zürich / (01)693388.

FARMS: **Bavarian Forest (Bayrische-Wald), W. Germany (Nava-Jīyada-Nṛsiṁha-Kṣetra)**—(contact ISKCON Munich); **Brihuega, Spain (New Vraja Maṇḍala)**—(Santa Clara) Brihuega, Guadalajara / (11) 280018; **Florence, Italy (Villa Vṛndāvana)**—Via Comunale degli Scopeti, No. 108, St. Andrea in Percussina, San Casciano Val di Pesa 56030 (Firenze) / 055-820054; **London, England**—(contact Bhaktivedanta Manor); **Valencay, France (New Mayapur)**—Lucay-Le-Male, 36 600 / (54) 40-23-26.

RESTAURANTS: **London**—Healthy, Wealthy, and Wise, 9-10 Soho Street / 01-437-1835; **Stockholm**—Govinda's, Grevgatan 18, 114 53 Stockholm / 08-623411; **Vienna**—Govinda (at ISKCON Vienna); **Zürich**—Govinda, Brandschenkestrasse 12, 8002 Zürich / (01)2029282.

AUSTRALASIA

Adelaide, Australia—13-A Frome St. / (08)223-2084; **Auckland, New Zealand**—Hwy. 18, Riverhead (next to Huapai Golfcourse) (mail: c/o R.D. 2, Kumeu) / 412-8075; **Brisbane, Australia**—56 Bellevue Terrace, St. Lucia 4066, Queensland; **Christchurch, New Zealand**—30 Latimer Sq.; **Jakarta, Indonesia**—Jalan Rawamangun Muka Timur 80 / 4835-19; **Lautoka, Fiji**—5 Tavewa Ave. (mail: c/o P.O. Box 125) / 61-633, ext. 48; **Melbourne, Australia**—197 Danks St., Albert Park, Melbourne, Victoria 3206 (mail: c/o P.O. Box 125) / 699-5122; **Perth, Australia**—P.O. Box 299, Subiaco, 6008, Perth, Western Australia; **Sydney, Australia**—112 Darlinghurst Rd., King's Cross, N.S.W. (mail: c/o P.O. Box 159) / (02)357-5162.

FARMS: **Auckland, New Zealand (New Varshana)**—contact ISKCON Auckland; **Colo, Australia (Bhaktivedanta Ashram)**—Upper Colo Rd., N.S.W. (mail: c/o P.O. Box 493, St. Mary's, 2760, N.S.W.) / 045-75-5284; **Murwillumbah, Australia (New Govardhana)**—'Eungella,' Tyalgum Rd. via Murwillumbah, N.S.W. 2484 (mail: c/o P.O. Box 687) / 066-72-1903.

RESTAURANTS: **Adelaide**—Govinda's, 13 Frome Street; **Melbourne**—Gopal's, 237 Flinders Lane / 63 1578; **Melbourne**—Gopal's, 251 Malvern Road, South Yarrow; **Sydney**—Mukunda's, 233 Victoria Street, Darlinghurst / 357 5162.

LATIN AMERICA

BRAZIL: **Curitiba, Paraná**—Rua Profa. Maria Assumpaco 77, Vila Hauer, 80.000 / 276-6274; **Pindamonhangaba, SP**—Rua Dom Joao Bosco 848, Santana; **Pôrto Alegre, RS**—Rua Giordano Bruno 318, 90.000; **Recife, Pernambuco**—Ave. 17 de Agosto 257, Parnamirim 50.000; **Rio de Janeiro, RJ**—Estrada dos Tres Rios 654, Jacarepagua, 22.700; **Salvador, Bahia**—Rua Alvaro Adorno 17, Brotas, 40.000 / (071)240-1072; **São Paulo, SP**—Rua Pandia Calogeras 54, 01525 / (011)270-3442.

FARM: **Pindamonhangaba, São Paulo (New Gokula)**—Ribeirao Grande (mail: C.P. 108, 12.400 Pindamonhangaba) / 2797836.

OTHER COUNTRIES: **Bogotá, Colombia**—Carrera 3A No. 54-A-72 / 255-9842; **Cuzco, Peru**—Avenida Pardo No. 1036 / 2277; **Georgetown, Guyana**—24 Uitvlugt Front, West Coast Demerara; **Guadalajara, Mexico**—Avenida las Americas No. 225, Sector Hidalgo / 163455; **Guatemala City, Guatemala**—Sexta Avenida 1-89, Zona 1 / 24618; **La Paz, Bolivia**—Calle Chacaltaya No. 587 / 32-85-67; **Lima, Peru**—Jiron Junin 415 / 47-18-10; **Medellin, Colombia**—Carrera 32, No. 54-42; **Mexico City, Mexico**—Gob. Tiburcio Montiel 45, San Miguel Chapultepec, Mexico D.F. 18 / (905)271-0132; **Monterrey, Mexico**—General Albino Espinoza, 345 Pte., Zona Centro, Monterrey, N.L. / 42 67 66; **Panama City, Panama**—43-58 Via España Altos, Al Lado del Cine, Bella Vista; **Puebla, Mexico**—Sierra Madre 9010, Colonia Maravillas, Puebla; **Quito, Ecuador**—Apdo. 2384, Calle Yasuni No. 404; **St. Augustine, Trinidad and Tobago**—Gordon St. at Santa Margarita Circular Rd. / 662-4605; **San José, Costa Rica**—400 mtrs. Sur Centro Médico de Guadalupe (casa blanca esquinera) Colonia Chapultepec, Guadalupe; **San Salvador, El Salvador**—67 Avenida Sur No. 115, Colonia Escalo; **Santiago, Chile**—Eyzaguirre 2404, Casilla 44, Puente Alto / 283; **Santo Domingo, Dominican Republic**—Calle Cayatano Rodriguez No. 254 / (809)688-7242; **Valparaiso, Chile**—Colon 2706 / 7099; **Vera Cruz, Mexico**—Calle 3 Carabelas No. 784, Fraccionmiento Reforma, Vera Cruz.

ASIA

INDIA: **Ahmedabad, Gujarat**—7, Kailas Society, Ashram Rd., 380 009 / 49935; **Bangalore, Mysore**—34/A, 9B Cross, West of Chord Rd., Rajajinagar 2nd Stage, 560 010; **Bhadrak, Orissa**—Gour Gopal Mandir, Kuans, P.O. Bhadrak, Dist. Balasore; **Bhubaneswar, Orissa**—National Highway No. 5, Nayapalli (mail: c/o P.O. Box 173, 751 001) / 53125; **Bombay, Maharastra**—Hare Krishna Land, Juhu, 400 049 / 566-860; **Calcutta, W. Bengal**—3 Albert Rd., 700 017 / 44-3757; **Chandigarh, Punjab**—Hare Krishna Land, Dakshin Marg, Sector 36-B, 160 023; **Chhaygharia (Haridaspur), W. Bengal**—Thakur Haridas Sripatbari Sevashram, P.O. Chhaygharia, P.S. Bongaon, Dist. 24 Pargonas; **Gauhati, Assam**—Post Bag No. 127, 781 001; **Hyderabad, A.P.**—Hare Krishna Land, Nampally Station Rd., 500 001 / 51018; **Imphal, Manipur**—Paona Bazar, 795 001; **Madras, Tamil Nadu**—4 Srinivasamurty Ave., Adayar, Madras 20; **Mayapur, W. Bengal**—Shree Mayapur Chandrodaya Mandir, P.O. Shree Mayapur Dham (District Nadia); **New Delhi, U.P.**—M-119 Greater Kailash 1, 110 048 / 624-590; **Patna, Bihar**—Post Bag 173, Patna 800 001; **Vrindavan, U.P.**—Krishna-Balarama Mandir, Bhaktivedanta Swami Marg, Raman Reti, Mathura / 178.

FARMS: **Hyderabad, A.P.**—P.O. Dabilpur Village, Medchal Taluq, Hyderabad District, 501 401; **Mayapur, W. Bengal**—(contact ISKCON Mayapur).

RESTAURANTS: **Bombay**—Hare Krishna Land; **Mayapur**—Shree Mayapur Chandrodaya Mandir; **Vrindavan**—Krishna-Balarama Mandir.

OTHER COUNTRIES: **Bangkok, Thailand**—P.O. Box 12-1108; **Butterworth, Malaysia**—1 Lintang Melur, M.K. 14, Butterworth, Province Wellesley / 04-331019; **Colombo, Sri Lanka**—188, New Chetty St., Colombo 13 / 33325; **Hong Kong**—5 Homantin St., Flat 23, Kowloon / 3-029113; **Kathmandu, Nepal**—8/6, Battis Putali, Goshalla; **Mandaue City, Philippines**—231 Pagsabungan Rd., Basak, Cebu / 83254; **Saitama-Ken, Japan**—3-2884-8 Higashisayanagaoka, Tokorozawa-shi, Saitama-Ken, Japan 359; **Selangor, Malaysia**—No. 18 Jalan 6/6, Petaling Jaya / 564957.

AFRICA

Durban (Natal), S. Africa—P.O. Box 212, Cato Ridge, Natal 3680 / Cato Ridge 237; **Johannesburg, S. Africa**—Elberta Rd., Honeydew (mail: P.O. Box 5302, Weltevreden Park 1715) / 6752845; **Lagos, Nigeria**—P.O. Box 8793, West Africa; **Mauritius**—10 E. Serret St., Rose Hill (mail: P.O. Box 718, Port Louis, Mauritius); **Mombasa, Kenya, E. Africa**—Madhavani House, Sauti Ya Kenya and Kisumu Rd., P.O. Box 82224 / 312248; **Nairobi, Kenya, E. Africa**—Puran Singh Close, P.O. Box 28946 / 331568.